DATE DUE

DEC 1 8 1987	
NOV 1 5 1989	
DEC 4 1989	
NOV 9 1990	
MAR 2 1991	
OCT 7 1991	
JUL 2 7 1992	
DEC 1 6 1994	
JUL 1 3 1998	
DEC 0 8 1999	
FEB 1 9 2002	
APR 1 8 2002	
OCT 1 5 2010	
DEC 1 1 2010	
MAY 1 6 2015	
FEB 1 4 2017	

TWENTIETH CENTURY VIEWS

The aim of this series is to present the best in contemporary critical opinion on major authors, providing a twentieth century perspective on their changing status in an era of profound revaluation.

Maynard Mack, *Series Editor*
Yale University

JAMES BALDWIN

JAMES BALDWIN

A COLLECTION OF CRITICAL ESSAYS

Edited by

Keneth Kinnamon

Prentice-Hall, Inc. Englewood Cliffs, N.J.

Library of Congress Cataloging in Publication Data

KINNAMON, KENETH, comp.
   James Baldwin; a collection of critical essays.

   (Twentieth century views) (A Spectrum Book)
   Bibliography: p.
   1. Baldwin, James, 1924–   —Criticism and
interpretation.
PS3552.A45Z76   818′.5′409   74–6175
ISBN 0–13–055566–5
ISBN 0–13–055558–4 (pbk.)

10   9   8   7   6   5

PRENTICE-HALL INTERNATIONAL, INC. (*London*)
PRENTICE-HALL OF AUSTRALIA, PTY. LTD. (*Sydney*)
PRENTICE-HALL OF CANADA, LTD. (*Toronto*)
PRENTICE-HALL OF INDIA PRIVATE LIMITED (*New Delhi*)
PRENTICE-HALL OF JAPAN, INC. (*Tokyo*)

To My Father

Acknowledgments

Quotations from the following works of James Baldwin are used by kind permission of The Dial Press and James Baldwin:

The Fire Next Time. Copyright © 1962, 1963 by James Baldwin.
Go Tell It on the Mountain. Copyright 1952, 1953 by James Baldwin.
Tell Me How Long the Train's Been Gone. Copyright © 1968 by James Baldwin.
Giovanni's Room. Copyright © 1956 by James Baldwin.
Another Country. Copyright © 1960, 1962 by James Baldwin.

Quotations from *No Name in the Street* by James Baldwin are used by kind permission of The Dial Press and James Baldwin. Copyright © 1972 by James Baldwin.

Contents

JAMES BALDWIN

Introduction

by Keneth Kinnamon

A decade ago James Baldwin, more than any other author, seemed to liberal white Americans to personify as well as to articulate the outrage and anguish of black Americans struggling to put an end to racial oppression and to achieve their civil and human rights. Two essays published in *The New Yorker* and *The Progressive* late in 1962 made a strong impression; when reprinted as *The Fire Next Time* early the following year, their impact was nothing short of phenomenal. Though as Northern as Martin Luther King was Southern, James Baldwin preached a more secular and apocalyptic but not really dissimilar sermon: the redemptive force of the love of a prophetic, interracial few could, even at that late date, yet prevail over the bigotry of the white majority, and so "end the racial nightmare, and achieve our country, and change the history of the world." If these brave words today seem both naïve and anachronistic, the reason is partly the nation's recent habit of giving more publicity than credence to its seers, of lavishing attention while withholding belief. America saw Baldwin's expressive face on the cover of *Time* and on the television screen, heard his words, read his books, but somehow the nightmare deepened, the ideal country was not realized, and the history of the world did not change, except, perhaps, for the worse. Although the capacity of white liberals to effect real change is debatable, the fact is that their efforts to do so tended more to expiatory gestures than to the requisite radical action.

But a failure of perception as well as a failure of nerve was involved, for James Baldwin was too exceptional to be wholly the black spokesman that many whites took him to be. The deprivations of his Harlem childhood were genuine enough to be representative, but otherwise he was quite atypical, this frail bohemian

I wish to acknowledge the aid of my research assistants, John Livingston and Isaac Brumfield, in gathering materials for this book.

1

intellectual who read Dickens, Stowe, and Stevenson as a boy, made his literary debut in Greenwich Village as a reviewer praising art and denouncing propaganda, and spent his middle and late twenties as an expatriate in Paris struggling with problems of racial and sexual identity. A proper understanding of Baldwin and his work must take into account a complicated amalgam of psychological and social elements sometimes thought to be antithetical. If, like most major black writers, Baldwin has extracted from his private ordeal the symbolic outline of his race's suffering, he has done so without obscuring the uniqueness of his personal experience.

II

Growing up in a squalid Harlem neighborhood, the scrawny young Baldwin was ill-equipped to cope with the poverty his family endured, the taunts of his schoolmates concerning his diminutive size and physical ugliness, the very real dangers of the streets. Still less was he psychologically prepared to handle the relentless hatred of his stepfather, David Baldwin, a tyrannical, paranoid laborer and storefront preacher, who married James's mother in 1927, accepting her illegitimate son only with the most grudging resentment. Shrinking from this man's hostility, James became all the more deeply attached to his mother, in an unmistakably Oedipal pattern. But he had to share Emma Baldwin's love with the eight half brothers and sisters born between 1927 and 1943. And since his mother had to work as a domestic to support this growing family, James himself, as the oldest, was forced to assume a maternal role toward them, changing their diapers, teaching them to walk, keeping them out of mischief. Needing desperately to receive love, he was constantly required to give it. A lonely child himself, he had to try to alleviate the loneliness of still younger children.

When older, Baldwin sought compensation in reading, in his studies generally, and in writing. His teachers, black and white, at Public School 24 and Frederick Douglass Junior High School in Harlem and at De Witt Clinton High School in the Bronx were impressed by his brilliance and his verbal facility. At Douglass, the famous poet Countee Cullen and another Harvard graduate named Herman W. Porter nourished Baldwin's literary ambitions during his tenure as editor of the school magazine, as did his white teachers at Clinton, where he edited *The Magpie*. The fiction, poetry, plays, and essays which poured from his pen during these years constituted, as he told Fern Marja Eckman in her biography *The Furious Passage of James Baldwin*, "an act of love. It was an attempt —not to get the world's attention—it was an attempt to be loved. It seemed a way to save myself and a way to save my family. It came out of despair. And it seemed the only way to another world."

Another route to salvation was through Mount Calvary of the Pentecostal Faith Church, whose pastor was a charismatic black woman called Mother Horn, the prototype of the protagonist of Baldwin's play *The Amen Corner*. Converted at the age of fourteen —a crucial event which Baldwin was to treat in both *Go Tell It on the Mountain* and *The Fire Next Time*—he quickly became a preacher in another storefront church, mounting the pulpit at least once weekly during his three years in high school. However much he may revile the historical role of Christianity in the enslavement of black people, *The Fire Next Time* attests that he has never forgotten the compensatory values of his religious experience: "In spite of everything, there was in the life I fled a zest and a joy and a capacity for facing and surviving disaster that are very moving and very rare." And for good or ill, Baldwin's work is of a kind in which the didactic—even homiletic—element is of the essence.

As a child in Harlem, Baldwin was relatively insulated from direct, personal contacts with white racism. Nevertheless, he did suffer harassment from white policemen, including a terrifying incident at the age of ten mentioned in *The Fire Next Time* and treated at length in *Tell Me How Long the Train's Been Gone*. But for the most part white oppression was an abstract force, responsible somehow for the poverty and desperation which surrounded him, the invisible cause of a visible result. Then, too, he had derived more benefit than harm from white teachers, especially the altruistic Orilla Miller at Public School 24, and from such white high school friends as Emile Capouya, Richard Avedon, and Sam Schulman. When he began work after graduation in the booming wartime economy of New Jersey, however, he was exposed to blatant racism, to what Richard Wright had called "The Ethics of Living Jim Crow." The full awareness of his white countrymen's racial feelings toward him brought with it what Baldwin in *Notes of a Native Son* has called a permanent disease whose syndrome includes "a kind of blind fever, a pounding in the skull and fire in the bowels." After his father's death in 1943, just before the race riot of the summer of that year, Baldwin concluded that for him neither Harlem nor New Jersey was habitable. As an aspiring writer, he thought that Greenwich Village might be.

But life was, if anything, even more frenetic for Baldwin in the Village than in Harlem or New Jersey. The basic problem seems to have been similar to that of the protagonist, an actor named Peter, in his first important short story, "Previous Condition." As a black man, he could not identify with a white racist society. As an artist-intellectual, he thought that he could not identify with black people. This double estrangement, together with the hectic pace of working by day and writing by night and his troubling questions of sexuality, intensified his nervous condition to an intolerable degree. If the United States offered no refuge, perhaps Europe would. Perhaps, as Richard Wright claimed, "There is more freedom in one square block of Paris than in all of the Unted States."

Baldwin had met Wright, his "idol since high school," in the winter of 1944–45, and the older man had bolstered his confidence by securing for him a Eugene F. Saxton Memorial Trust Award to work on his first novel. Other important contacts followed with such editors as Robert Warshaw of *Commentary* and Philip Rahv of *Partisan Review*. Some seventeen pieces by Baldwin, mostly reviews, appeared in these magazines and in *The Nation* and *The New Leader* between April 12, 1947, and November 11, 1948, when he sailed for France to begin what he vowed would be a permanent expatriation. Thoroughly exasperated with the United States and encountering difficulties with his efforts at long fiction, he had nevertheless established his name among New York intellectuals, who would welcome enthusiastically the publication of *Go Tell It on the Mountain* five years later. His apprenticeship was not over, but he could call himself a writer.

If not the sanctuary it seemed from New York, Paris had certain compensations for Baldwin, chief of which was the love he found with Lucien Happersberger. Paris and the south of France provide the setting for his second published novel, *Giovanni's Room*. But Baldwin never became a Francophile, as the essay "Equal in Paris" attests, and his restlessness could not in any case be contained by a single city. For the last two decades his itinerary has included Switzerland, New York, Africa, Puerto Rico, Istanbul, London, Hamburg, Los Angeles, and many other way stations. During the late fifties and early sixties, his commitment to the civil rights movement took him to the "old country"—the American South—and to college campuses across the land.

In spite of his perpetual movement, his impulsive involvements with causes and individuals, and his status as a celebrity, his literary productivity has been considerable. At age fifty, Baldwin is the author of four novels, four collections of essays, a collection of short stories, two plays and a screenplay, two books of recorded conversations, and a sizable body of miscellaneous writing. And it seems certain that much good work lies ahead.

III

Out of Baldwin's experience have emerged certain recurring themes in his writing, the most important of which is the quest for love. On a personal level, the search is for the emotional security of a love of which the protagonist has always been deprived. In his brilliant first novel, *Go Tell It on the Mountain,* the theme develops with autobiographical clarity, as is also the case in the related short story "The Outing" or such essays as "Notes of a Native Son," "The Black Boy Looks at the White Boy," "Down at the Cross," and "No Name in the Street." But elsewhere the search for love is equally imperative. David finds it in *Giovanni's Room* but loses it again because of his failure to commit himself totally. The interracial and bisexual bedhopping of *Another Country* constitutes a frenzied effort to realize love in the loveless city of New York. It falls to Leo Proudhammer of *Tell Me How Long the Train's Been Gone* to articulate the poignant paradox of Baldwin's love theme: "Everyone wishes to be loved, but, in the event, nearly no one can bear it. Everyone desires love but also finds it impossible to believe that he deserves it." If the search for love has its origin in the desire of a child for emotional security, its arena is an adult world which involves it in struggle and pain. Stasis must yield to motion, innocence to experience, security to risk. This is the lesson that the black Ida inculcates in her white lover Vivaldo in *Another Country,* and it saves Baldwin's central fictional theme from sentimentality.

Similarly, love as an agent of racial reconciliation and national survival is not for Baldwin a vague yearning for an innocuous brotherhood, but an agonized confrontation with reality, leading to the struggle to transform it. It is a quest for truth through a recognition of the primacy of suffering and injustice in the American past. In racial terms, the black man as victim of this past is in a moral position to induce the white man, the oppressor, to end his self-delusion and begin the process of regeneration. "And if the word *integration* means anything," Baldwin wrote in 1962 in "My Dungeon Shook," "this is what it means: that we, with love, shall force our brothers to see themselves as they are, to cease fleeing from reality and begin to change it." By 1972, the year of *No Name in the Street,* the redemptive possibilities of love seemed exhausted in that terrible decade of assassination, riot, and repression, of the Black Panthers and Attica. Social love had now become for Baldwin more a rueful memory than an alternative to disaster. Violence, he now believes, is the arbiter of history, and in its matrix the white world is dying and the third world is struggling to be born. In his fiction, too, this shift in emphasis is apparent. Though love may still be a sustaining personal force, its social utility is dubious. At the end of *Tell Me How Long the Train's Been Gone,* the young militant instructs the middle-aged protagonist in the new reality: " 'Guns,' said Christopher. 'We need guns.' " Thus for Baldwin a terrible beauty is born.

Whether through the agency of love or violence, Baldwin is almost obsessively concerned with the writer's responsibility to save the world. As an essayist, he assumes the burden not only of reporting with eloquent sensitivity his observations of reality, but also of tirelessly reminding us of the need to transform that reality if Armageddon is to be averted. Over and over he concludes an essay by enlarging the perspective to a global scale. Thus "Many Thousands Gone," a piece on *Native Son,* ends with a warning against the danger of "surrendering to those forces which reduce the person to anonymity and which make themselves manifest daily all over the darkening world." The autobiographical account of his imbroglio with French police in "Equal in Paris" leads to the chilling recognition that the mocking laughter directed toward the unfortunate by the comfortable and secure is not local but "universal and never can be stilled." From his personal sojourn high in the Swiss Alps as a "Stranger in the Village," he extrapolates the concluding message of *Notes of a Native Son*: "This world is white no longer, and it will never be white again." Introducing the theme of self-examination in *Nobody Knows My Name,* he asserts that "one can only face in others what one can face in oneself. On this confrontation depends the measure of our wisdom and compassion. This energy is all that one finds in the rubble of vanished civilizations, and the only hope for ours." This relationship between the subjective vision and the external world is repeated at the end of "The Discovery of What It Means to Be an American," where he claims that "Though we do not wholly believe it yet, the interior life is a real life, and the intangible dreams of people have a tangible effect on the world." Commenting on demonstrations at the United Nations in protest of the death of Patrice Lumumba, he warns in the last sentence of "East River, Downtown": "If we are not able, and quickly, to face and begin to eliminate the sources of this discontent in our own country, we will never be able to do it on the great stage of the world." Unless honest personal and national self-examination is made, he further declares at the end of the title piece of his second collection of essays, "we may yet become one of the most distinguished and monumental failures in the history of nations." Two of the simplest expressions of his faith in the possibility of change are the concluding challenges of the speeches entitled "In Search of a Majority" and "Notes for a Hypothetical Novel": "The world is before you and you need not take it or leave it as it was when you came in" and "We made the world we're living in and we have to make it over." *Nobody Knows My Name* concludes with an account of Baldwin's friendship with Norman Mailer, another writer who emphasizes the social value of the literary perspective: "For, though it clearly needs to be brought into focus, he has a real vision of ourselves as we are, and it cannot be too often repeated in this country now, that, where there is no vision, the people perish." The possibility of just such a perishing is pursued further in *The Fire Next Time,* and the possibility has become a probability in *No Name in the Street,* where Baldwin speaks of "the shape of the wrath to come" and the setting of the white man's sun.

As a writer, then, James Baldwin has always been concerned with the most personal and intimate areas of experience and also with the broadest questions of national and global destiny—and with the intricate interrelationships between the two. Whatever the final assessment of his literary achievement, it is clear that his voice—simultaneously that of victim, witness, and prophet—has been among the most urgent of our time.

IV

With his deep interest in the most debatable issues of personality, race, and history, Baldwin has deliberately sought controversy, and his work has elicited in turn the most diverse critical opinions. The issues of this body of criticism are sharply focused. One concerns the old question of art versus propaganda. Does Baldwin sacrifice "universality" to his desire to portray with fidelity black life-styles and to protest against white racism? Some white critics would argue that he does, but this view is advanced less insistently today than it was in the past. Far from overemphasizing black uniqueness, some black critics maintain, Baldwin has been so deeply influenced by white literary and social values as to make him an increasingly anachronistic literary spokesman for integration. In either case, a further question persists. Given the consensus judgment that *Giovanni's Room, Another Country,* and *Tell Me How Long the Train's Been Gone* are less fully achieved works of fiction than *Go Tell It on the Mountain,* is it fair to say that Baldwin is essentially an essayist rather than a novelist? Or do his last three novels fail because they exploit sensationalism? Then, there is the problem of Baldwin's style. Praising him as "one of the best writers that we have," Edmund Wilson claims that "he has mastered a taut and incisive style." Mark Schorer agrees that "we have hardly a more accomplished prose stylist in the United States today," while Charles Newman places him in the tradition of Henry James. On the other hand, Richard Gilman's objections to *Tell Me How Long the Train's Been Gone* are mainly on stylistic grounds, and other commentators have complained of a pseudopoetic floridity and reliance on clichés.

These and other issues are reflected in the essays gathered in this collection. The editor has made a deliberate effort to represent the diversity of perspective, approach, and conclusion that characterizes Baldwin criticism. Some essays provide an overview of Baldwin's literary career or his work in one genre; others trace a theme through several works; others analyze closely a single work or respond to its social implications. All the essays included, the editor believes, evince the excitement that Baldwin's work generates and that the reader is invited to share.

From Harlem to Paris

by *Langston Hughes*

I think that one definition of the great artist might be the creator who projects the biggest dream in terms of the least person. There is something in Cervantes or Shakespeare, Beethoven or Rembrandt or Louis Armstrong that millions can understand. The American native son who signs his name James Baldwin is quite a ways off from fitting such a definition of a great artist in writing, but he is not as far off as many another writer who deals in picture captions or journalese in the hope of capturing and retaining a wide public. James Baldwin writes down to nobody, and he is trying very hard to write up to himself. As an essayist he is thought-provoking, tantalizing, irritating, abusing and amusing. And he uses words as the sea uses waves, to flow and beat, advance and retreat, rise and take a bow in disappearing.

In "Notes of a Native Son," James Baldwin surveys in pungent commentary certain phases of the contemporary scene as they relate to the citizenry of the United States, particularly Negroes. Harlem, the protest novel, bigoted religion, the Negro press and the student milieu of Paris are all examined in black and white, with alternate shutters clicking, for hours of reading interest. When the young man who wrote this book comes to a point where he can look at life purely as himself, and for himself, the color of his skin mattering not at all, when, as in his own words, he finds "his birthright as a man no less than his birthright as a black man," America and the world might well have a major contemporary commentator.

Few American writers handle words more effectively in the essay form than James Baldwin. To my way of thinking, he is much better at provoking thought in the essay than he is in arousing emotion in fiction. I much prefer "Notes of a Native Son" to his novel, "Go

Tell It on the Mountain," where the surface excellence and poetry of his writing did not seem to me to suit the earthiness of his subject-matter. In his essays, words and material suit each other. The thought becomes poetry, and the poetry illuminates the thought.

What James Baldwin thinks of the protest novel from "Uncle Tom's Cabin" to Richard Wright, of the motion picture "Carmen Jones," of the relationships between Jews and Negroes, and of the problems of American minorities in general is herein graphically and rhythmically set forth. And the title chapter concerning his father's burial the day after the Harlem riots, heading for the cemetery through broken streets—"To smash something is the ghetto's chronic need"—is superb. That Baldwin's viewpoints are half American, half Afro-American, incompletely fused, is a hurdle which Baldwin himself realizes he still has to surmount. When he does, there will be a straight-from-the-shoulder writer, writing about the troubled problems of this troubled earth with an illuminating intensity that should influence for the better all who ponder on the things books say.

James Baldwin and the "Man"

by F. W. Dupee

As a writer of polemical essays on the Negro question James Baldwin has no equals. He probably has, in fact, no real competitors. The literary role he has taken on so deliberately and played with so agile an intelligence is one that no white writer could possibly imitate and that few Negroes, I imagine, would wish to embrace *in toto*. Baldwin impresses me as being the Negro *in extremis*, a virtuoso of ethnic suffering, defiance and aspiration. His role is that of the man whose complexion constitutes his fate, and not only in a society poisoned by prejudice but, it sometimes seems, in general. For he appears to have received a heavy dose of existentialism; he is at least half-inclined to see the Negro question in the light of the Human Condition. So he wears his color as Hester Prynne did her scarlet letter, proudly. And like her he converts this thing, in itself so absurdly material, into a form of consciousness, a condition of spirit. Believing himself to have been branded as different from and inferior to the white majority, he will make a virtue of his situation. He will *be* different and in his own way be better.

His major essays—for example, those collected in *Notes of a Native Son*—show the extent to which he is able to be different and in his own way better. Most of them were written, as other such pieces generally are, for the magazines, some obviously on assignment. And their subjects—a book, a person, a locale, an encounter—are the inevitable subjects of magazine essays. But Baldwin's way with them is far from inevitable. To apply criticism "in depth" to *Uncle Tom's Cabin* is, for him, to illuminate not only a book, an author, an age, but a whole strain in a country's culture. Similarly with those routine themes, the Paris expatriate and Life With Father, which he treats in "Equal In Paris" and the title piece of

"James Baldwin and the 'Man'" by F. W. Dupee. From *The New York Review of Books*, 1, no. 1 (1963), 1–2. Reprinted with permission from *The New York Review of Books*. Copyright © 1963 NYREV, Inc.

Notes of a Native Son, and which he wholly transfigures. Of course the transfiguring process in Baldwin's essays owes something to the fact that the point of view is a Negro's, an outsider's, just as the satire of American manners in *Lolita* and *Morte d'Urban* depends on their being written from the angle of, respectively, a foreign-born creep and a Catholic priest. But Baldwin's point of view in his essays is not merely that of the generic Negro. It is, as I have said, that of a highly stylized Negro, a role which he plays with an artful and zestful consistency and which he expresses in a language distinguished by clarity, brevity, and a certain formal elegance. He is in love, for example, with syntax, with sentences that mount through clearly articulated stages to a resounding and clarifying climax and then gracefully subside. For instance this one, from *The Fire Next Time*:

> Girls, only slightly older than I was, who sang in the choir or taught Sunday school, the children of holy parents, underwent, before my eyes, their incredible metamorphosis, of which the most bewildering aspect was not their budding breasts or their rounding behinds but something deeper and more subtle, in their eyes, their heat, their odor, and the inflection of their voices.

Nobody else in democratic America writes sentences like this anymore. It suggests the ideal prose of an ideal literary community, some aristocratic France of one's dreams. This former Harlem boy has undergone his own incredible metamorphosis.

His latest book, *The Fire Next Time,* differs in important ways from his earlier work in the essay. Its subjects are less concrete, less clearly defined; to a considerable extent he has exchanged prophecy for criticism, exhortation for analysis, and the results for his mind and style are in part disturbing. *The Fire Next Time* gets its title from a slave song: "God gave Noah the rainbow sign,/No more water the fire next time." But this small book with the incendiary title consists of two independent essays, both in the form of letters. One is a brief affair entitled "My Dungeon Shook" and addressed to "My Nephew on the One Hundredth Anniversary of the Emancipation." The ominous promise of this title is fulfilled in the text. Between the hundred-year-old anniversary and the fifteen-year-old nephew the disparity is too great even for a writer of Baldwin's rhetorical powers. The essay reads like some specimen of "public speech" as practiced by MacLeish or Norman Corwin. It is not good Baldwin.

The other, much longer, much more significant essay appeared first in a pre-Christmas number of *The New Yorker*, where it made, understandably, a sensation. It is called "Down At the Cross; Letter From a Region of My Mind." The subtitle should be noted. Evidently the essay is to be taken as only a partial or provisional declaration on Baldwin's part, a single piece of his mind. Much of it, however, requires no such appeal for caution on the reader's part. Much of it is unexceptionably first-rate. For example, the reminiscences of the writer's boyhood, which form the lengthy introduction. Other of Baldwin's writings have made us familiar with certain aspects of his Harlem past. Here he concentrates on quite different things: the boy's increasing awareness of the abysmally narrow world of choice he inhabits as a Negro, his attempt to escape a criminal existence by undergoing a religious conversion and becoming at fifteen a revivalist preacher, his discovery that he must learn to "inspire fear" if he hopes to survive the fear inspired in him by "the man"—the white man.

In these pages we come close to understanding why he eventually assumed his rather specialized literary role. It seems to have grown naturally out of his experience of New York City. As distinct from a rural or small-town Negro boy, who is early and firmly taught his place, young Baldwin knew the treacherous fluidity and anonymity of the metropolis, where hidden taboos and unpredictable animosities lay in wait for him and a trip to the 42nd Street Library could be a grim adventure. All this part of the book is perfect; and when Baldwin finally gets to what is his ostensible subject, the Black Muslims or Nation of Islam movement, he is very good too. As good, that is, as possible considering that his relations with the movement seem to have been slight. He once shared a television program with Malcolm X, "the movement's second-in-command," and he paid a brief and inconclusive visit to the first-in-command, the Honorable Elijah Muhammad, and his entourage at the party's headquarters in Chicago. (Muhammad ranks as a prophet; to him the Black Muslim doctrines were "revealed by Allah Himself.") Baldwin reports the Chicago encounter in charming detail and with what looks like complete honesty. On his leaving the party's rather grand quarters, the leader insisted on providing him with a car and driver to protect

him "from the white devils until he gets wherever it is he is going."
Baldwin accepted, he tells us, adding wryly: "I was, in fact, going to
have a drink with several white devils on the other side of town."

He offers some data on the Black Muslim movement, its aims and
finances. But he did a minimum of homework here. Had he done
more he might at least have provided a solid base for the speculative
fireworks the book abounds in. To cope thoroughly with the fireworks in short space, or perhaps any space, seems impossible. Ideas
shoot from the book's pages as the sparks fly upward, in bewildering
quantity and at random. I don't mean that it is all dazzle. On the
cruel paradoxes of the Negro's life, the failures of Christianity, the
relations of Negro and Jew, Baldwin is often superb. But a lot of
damage is done to his argument by his indiscriminate raids on
Freud, Lawrence, Sartre, Genet and other psychologists, metaphysi-
cians and melodramatists. Still more damage is done by his refusal
to draw on anyone so humble as Martin Luther King and his fellow-
practitioners of non-violent struggle.

For example: "White Americans do not believe in death, and this
is why the darkness of my skin so intimidates them." But suppose
one or two white Americans are *not* intimidated. Suppose someone
coolly asks what it means to "believe in death." Again: "Do I really
want to be integrated into a burning house?" Since you have no
other, yes; and the better-disposed firemen will welcome your as-
sistance. Again: "A vast amount of the energy that goes into what
we call the Negro problem is produced by the white man's profound
desire not to be judged by those who are not white." You exaggerate
the white man's consciousness of the Negro. Again: "The real reason that non-violence is considered to be a virtue in Negroes . . .
is that white men do not want their lives, their self-image, or their
property threatened." Of course they don't, especially their lives.
Moreover, this imputing of "real reasons" for the behavior of entire
populations is self-defeating, to put it mildly. One last quotation,
this time a regular apocalypse:

> In order to survive as a human, moving, moral weight in the world,
> America and all the Western nations will be forced to reexamine
> themselves and release themselves from many things that are now
> taken to be sacred, and to discard nearly all the assumptions that have
> been used to justify their lives and their anguish and their crimes so
> long.

Since whole cultures have never been known to "discard nearly all their assumptions" and yet remain intact, this amounts to saying that any essential improvement in Negro-white relations, and thus in the quality of American life, is unlikely.

So much for the fireworks. What damage, as I called it, do they do to the writer and his cause—which is also the concern of plenty of others? When Baldwin replaces criticism with prophecy, he manifestly weakens his grasp of his role, his style, and his great theme itself. And to what end? Who is likely to be moved by such arguments, unless it is the more literate Black Muslims, whose program Baldwin specifically rejects as both vindictive and unworkable. And with the situation as it is in Mississippi and elsewhere—dangerous, that is, to the Negro struggle and the whole social order—is not a writer of Baldwin's standing obliged to submit his assertions to some kind of pragmatic test, some process whereby their truth or untruth will be gauged according to their social utility? He writes: "The Negroes of this country may never be able to rise to power, but they are very well placed indeed to precipitate chaos and ring down the curtain on the American dream." I should think that the anti-Negro extremists were even better placed than the Negroes to precipitate chaos, or at least to cause a lot of trouble; and it is unclear to me how *The Fire Next Time,* in its madder moments, can do anything except inflame the former and confuse the latter. Assuming that a *book* can do anything to either.

Baldwin and the Problem of Being

by George E. Kent

In a *New York Times Book Review* essay, James Baldwin has stated that the effort to become a great novelist "involves attempting to tell as much of the truth as one can bear, and then a little more." [1] It is likely in our time to mean attacking much that Americans tend to hold sacred, in order that reality be confronted and constructively altered. As stated in "Everybody's Protest Novel," it means devotion to the "human being, his freedom and fulfillment; freedom which cannot be legislated, fulfillment which cannot be charted." [2] Baldwin then wishes to confront and affect the human consciousness and conscience. He rejects the tradition of the protest novel because he feels that it denies life, "the human being . . . his beauty, dread, power," and insists "that it is categorization alone which is real and which cannot be transcended." [3] He tries to write the way jazz musicians sound, to reflect their compassion,[4] and it is noteworthy that Baldwin's tendency in *Go Tell It on the Mountain* and *Another Country* is to focus upon the individual characters' experiences in a way similar to Ralph Ellison's description of Jazz:

> For true jazz is an art of individual assertion within and against the group. Each true jazz moment (as distinct from the uninspired commercial performance) springs from a contest in which each artist challenges all the rest; each solo flight or improvisation, represents

"Baldwin and the Problem of Being" by George E. Kent. From *CLA Journal*, 7, no. 3 (1964), 202–14. Copyright © 1964 by the College Language Association. Reprinted by permission of the College Language Association and the author.

1 James Baldwin, "As Much Truth As One Can Bear," *The New York Times Book Review* (January 14, 1962), p. 1.

2 *Notes of a Native Son* (Boston, 1955), p. 15.

3 *Ibid.*, p. 23.

4 "What's the Reason Why: A Symposium by Best Selling Authors," *The New York Times Book Review* (December 2, 1962), p. 3.

... a definition of his identity, as member of the collectivity, and as a link in the chain of tradition.[5]

It should be generally observed that Baldwin's writings owe much to Negro folk tradition (the blues, jazz, spirituals, and folk literature), and to the chief experimental practioneers of modernist fiction, with especial emphasis upon Henry James.

The moral vision that emerges is one primarily concerned with man as he relates to good and evil and to society. For there is evil in human nature and evil abroad in the world to be confronted, not through Christianity whose doctrine tends to be the perverted tool of the ruling classes and groups whose bankruptcy was registered by the slaughter of the Jews during the Third Reich,[6] but through the love and involvement available from those able to eat of the tree of the knowledge of good and evil and live. Within the breast of each individual, then, rages a universe of forces with which he must become acquainted, often through the help of an initiated person, in order to direct them for the positive growth of himself and others. The foregoing achievement is what Baldwin means by *identity*. To achieve it, one must not be hindered by the detritus of society and one must learn to know detritus when one sees it.

Perhaps the question which throws most light upon Baldwin's works is simply: How can one achieve, amid the dislocations and disintegrations of the modern world, true, functional being? For Baldwin, the Western concept of reality, with its naive rationalism, its ignoring of unrational forces that abound within and without man, its reductivist activities wherein it ignores the uniqueness of the individual and sees reality in terms of its simplifications and categorizations, is simply impoverishing. He who follows it fails to get into his awareness the richness and complexity of experience—he fails to be. And freedom is unattainable, since paradoxically, freedom is discovery and recognition of limitations, one's own and that of one's society;[7] to deny complexity is to paralyze the ability to get at such knowledge—it is to strangle freedom.

Groping unsteadily amidst the reductivist forces is an America which does not achieve, therefore, its primitive and essential moral

[5] Ralph Ellison, "The Charlie Christian Story," *Saturday Review of Literature* (May 17, 1958), p. 42.

[6] James Baldwin, *The Fire Next Time* (New York, 1963), p. 66.

[7] "James Baldwin: An Interview," *WMFT Perspective* (December, 1961), p. 37.

identity. For the great vision that motivated the American adventure, there has been substituted a quest for spurious glory in mass production and consumption. And yet, ". . . there is so much more than Cadillacs, Frigidaires, and IBM machines. . . . One of the things wrong with this country is this notion that IBM machines *prove* something." [8] Still until America achieves its moral identity, its people, whether white or black, can fulfill nothing.

The struggle for identity, i.e., for functional being, is the major issue of Baldwin's first novel, *Go Tell It on the Mountain*. Attempting to tell part of the story found in the Negro's music, which "Americans are able to admire because a protective sentimentality limits their understanding of it," [9] Baldwin examines three generations of a Negro family whose life span extends from slavery to the present day. The novel investigates, with warmth and perception, the Negro's possibility of achieving identity through the discipline of Christianity. The style is richly evocative, and one hears echoes of Joyce and Faulkner, the rhythms of the old time Negro sermon and the King James Bible. Unfolding in a series of major movements, the story proceeds as follows: the first movement introducing the reach of fourteen year old John Grimes for identity, a fearful, faltering reach, from a boy filled with guilt, hatred, fear, love, amidst the stern, religious frustrations of his elders and the pagan rebelliousness of his brother, Roy; the second presenting the tragedy of Florence, unable to overcome, among other things, the concept of the Negro she has internalized from the dominant culture—and therefore on insecure terms with herself and others; the third presenting Gabriel Grimes, stepfather of John, blocked from complete fulfillment by his attempts to escape his pagan drives in a fierce, frustrated embrace of Christianity; the fourth presenting Elizabeth, Mother of John, who after brief fulfillment in illicit love, retreats, frightened and awestricken, into the frustrated and frustrating arms of Gabriel Grimes. The final movement is the questionable flight of John Grimes from the quest for identity into the ostensible safety of religious ecstasy.

Vitally represented through a series of scenes occurring on his fourteenth birthday, reflected through images of poetic intensity, are the conflicts of young John. He stands upon a hill in New York's Central Park and feels "like a giant who might crumble this

[8] *Ibid.*
[9] *Notes of a Native Son*, p. 24.

city with his anger . . . like a tyrant who might crush this city with his heel . . . like a long awaited conqueror at whose feet flowers would be strewn, and before whom multitudes cried, Hosanna!" [10] Or concerning the rewards to be inherited from his preacher father: ". . . a house like his father's, a church like his father's, and a job like his father's, where he would grow old and black with hunger and toil. The way of the cross had given him a belly filled with wind and had bent his mother's back. . . ." [11] Mixed with his vision and perverting it is John's guilt over his sexual drives, the religious concept of the city as evil and the fatal tempter of the soul, and his parents' feeling that the city (New York) is filled with antagonistic whites who will block the worldly aspirations of Negroes. Over such obstacles John peers, enveloped in a solitude that seems well nigh unbreakable.

Part II, containing the stories of the adult members of the family who came to manhood and womanhood at the time of Emancipation, begins powerfully. Passionate scenes reveal the problems with which each character struggles. For Florence, the sister of the minister Gabriel, the central problem is to achieve an identity that excludes the concubinage already offered by her white Southern employer, the general sexual opportunism, or the image of the toil blasted bearer of children with its attendant heritage—a cabin like her mother's. In addition, Florence is one of a long line of Baldwin's characters who have absorbed from the dominant culture the concept of blackness as low, contemptible, evil. Baldwin has said, "The American image of the Negro lives also in the Negro's heart; and when he has surrendered to this image life has no other possible reality." [12] Controlled by such an image, Florence founders in a mixture of self-hatred, self-righteousness, sadism, and guilt feelings. Married to a ne'er-do-well she succeeds merely in outraging herself and him, and in driving him away. She bows to religious ecstasy. Baldwin's point, of course, is that she was unable to achieve a life affirming love or her potential identity, and that her ecstatic surrender to Christianity as she nears the end of life is a gesture of desperation.

A man of titanic drives, Gabriel is a sufficient metaphor for man in a grim struggle with the forces of the universe; he stops just short

---

[10] *Go Tell It on the Mountain* (New York, 1953), p. 35.
[11] *Ibid.*, p. 37.
[12] *Notes*, p. 38.

of evoking the sense of tragedy, since self-recognition is not clearly confessed. What is available for articulating the self amid these forces, however, is a version of St. Paul's Christianity which assures the self a Pyrrhic victory by a repression that carries the mere coloring of a humanistic morality. Since sex, for Baldwin, is obviously a metaphor for the act of breaking one's isolation and, properly experienced, responsibly entering into the complexity of another human being, Gabriel's evasion of it by marrying the sexless Deborah (symbolically enough, mass raped by Southern whites and sterile) is his flight from dealing with his humanity. Baldwin contrasts him well with the pagan Esther, by whom a temporarily backsliding Gabriel begets a child he does not acknowledge. Esther has a firm concept of her dignity and humanity, and what is life-affirming and what is life-negating, and some of his fellow ministers, too, show that they do not take their fundamentalist concepts to rigid conclusions. Gabriel's response is to retreat more fiercely into religion, marry, after the death of Deborah, the fallen Elizabeth, and harden in his grotesqueness.

Elizabeth is the ethical and moral center of the book. It is through her attachment to her father and reaction against her mother and aunt that she gains the sense of a love that is life giving. She knows that love's imprisonment is not a "bribe, a threat, an indecent will to power"; it is "mysteriously, a freedom for the soul and spirit . . . water in the dry places." [13] It seems to me, however, that Baldwin's hand falters in his analysis and presentation of her as a young woman. Her important relationship with her father, to the extent that it is at all rendered, is simply that of the conventional petting and "spoiling" afforded by a loose living man who does not take his fatherhood very seriously. That is to say that the father's free loving nature binds him to nothing, and, after cautioning Elizabeth (as we learn through a summary) never to let the world see her suffering, he returns to his job of running a house of prostitution. Amidst the religious illusions of the other characters, however, she retains a strong, quiet sense of her integrity, despite a relative commitment to religious passion.

Her fall came through her common-law husband, Richard, to whom she gave a self-sacrificial, life creating love. Although the portrayal of Richard as victimized by society and as a man whose

---

[13] *Go Tell It on the Mountain*, p. 210.

being cannot fulfill its hunger is moving, the explanation of his curiosity and hunger seems oversimplified, if not, indeed, dehumanized: ". . . that I was going to get to know everything them white bastards knew . . . so could no white son-of-a-bitch *nowhere* never talk *me* down, and never make me feel like *I* was dirt. . . ." [14] Although the statement well reflects Richard's sensitivity and insecurity under the racial system of America, it hardly explains "his great adoration for things dead."

After the proud young Richard kills himself in reaction to extreme humiliation by the police who have imposed upon his consciousness the image of the low bestial Negro that he has tried to escape, Elizabeth gives birth to the bastard John, whose quest for identity forms the central movement of the book. As the second wife of Gabriel, she emerges as a person of complexity, and is sensitively involved in John's reach for life.

By a series of flashbacks, the author keeps us mindful that the present involves John Grimes's search for identity, the achievement of which is to be understood within the context of the lives of his elders. In the last section of the story, he is in crisis, and with the help of his friend Elisha, in a religious ecstasy, commits himself to the Cross. At various points, Baldwin uses a character by whose views the reality witnessed is to be qualified. In addition to the foreshadowings scattered throughout the story, there is Gabriel to point out that the ecstatic conversion is still to be tested by the long, complex journey of life. So quite without surprise, we encounter in a later short story, "The Death of the Prophet," an apostate Johnny who returns guiltily from some place of estrangement almost to collapse in the presence of his dying father.

That Baldwin in *Go Tell It on the Mountain* has drawn heavily upon autobiographical experiences is obvious, and those who like the pursuit can make interesting parallels with autobiographical situations reported in the essay collections: *Notes of a Native Son*, *Nobody Knows My Name*, and *The Fire Next Time*. But, from the artistic point of view, what is more interesting is their transmutation, their representation as organized energies that carry mythic force in their reflection of man attempting to deal with destiny. Much power derives from the confrontation of the ambiguity of life. That ambiguity carries into the various attitudes suggested

---

14 *Ibid.*, pp. 225–226.

toward the version of Christianity that his characters relate themselves to. The relatively non-religious characters do not deny the
relevance of God but seem to feel as Esther, the spurned mother of
Gabriel's illegitimate child, puts it: ". . . that [the Lord's] spirit
ain't got to work in everybody the same, seems to me." [15] Of the
religiously engrossed characters, only Elizabeth achieves a relatively
selfless being. However, the religion sustained the slave mother of
Gabriel. Even for the twisted, it is a place of refuge, an articulation
of the complexity of the mysterious forces of a demanding universe.
But finally, the religion only partially illuminates, and the characters must grope in its light and bump against forces within and
without that the religion has merely hidden or dammed.

With some admitted oversimplifications inescapable in tracing
thematic lines, it may be said that in his two succeeding novels
Baldwin is preoccupied with sex and love as instruments in the
achievement of full being. As a novelist still under forty, he is no
doubt creating works important to his total development, but in
neither of these novels—*Giovanni's Room* and the best seller *Another Country*—does he seem to fully create his fictional worlds and
characters; in short, he does not seem to have found characters who
release his very real ability to create.

In an essay "Preservation of Innocence," Baldwin explicitly makes
his criticism of popular concepts of sexuality. His chief point is that
our rational classifications of sexual characteristics and our efforts
to preserve conventional norms tell us little about what it means
to be a man or a woman. Our classifications are not definitive, and
therefore we panic and set up safeguards that do nothing more
than guard against sexual activities between members of the same
sex. But such reductive simplicity, he argues, guarantees ignorance
merely, or worse the probability that the bride and groom will not
be able to add to the sum of love or know each other since they do
not know themselves. Whatever position one takes regarding the
argument, the following statements shed uncomfortable light upon
the relationship between the sexes in much of American fiction:

> In the truly awesome attempt of the American to at once preserve
> his innocence and arrive at man's estate, that mindless monster, the
> tough guy, has been created and perfected, whose masculinity is
> found in the most infantile and elementary externals and whose

attitude towards women is the wedding of the most abysmal romanticism and the most implacable distrust.[16]

Further complaint of the reductive approach to sexuality is contained in a review of André Gide's *Madeleine,* in which he describes the possibility of communing with another sex as "the door to life and air and freedom from the tyranny of one's own personality. . . ."[17] And he describes our present day as one in which communion between the sexes "has become so sorely threatened that we depend more and more on the strident exploitation of externals, as, for example, the breasts of Hollywood glamor girls and the mindless grunting and swaggering of Hollywood he-men."[18] Despite our claim to knowledge, Baldwin implies, sex is a mystery that each person must find a way to live with.

In the light of the foregoing, it seems to me, Baldwin's intention in the novel *Giovanni's Room,* is more easily understood. The main line of the story portrays the way a youth's inherited definitions of sexuality fail him in his attempts to come to terms with his own, and adds to the sum of evil in his relationship with others. The chief character David represents the rational Westerner, who has absorbed the simplified, compartmentalized thinking of his background. Falling first in a romantic homosexual experience with a fellow adolescent, Joey, he experiences that escape from isolation and the heightened spiritual awareness which love is supposed to bring. However, "A cavern opened in my mind, black, full of rumor, suggestion . . . I could have cried, cried for shame and terror, cried for not understanding how this could have happened to me, how this could have happened in me."[19] Unresolved oedipal conflicts are hinted, and just when he needs spiritual sustenance from a father, his father, who knows nothing of the son's experience, insists upon retaining the simplified concept of himself as his son's "buddy." In flight from Joey, David repeats the mishap in the army, then takes flight to France to "find himself," but once there tentatively enters into a similar relationship with Giovanni. David expects Giovanni to be but an interval in life, since David has also a girlfriend Hella, a very rational minded girl who has gone to Spain to think out whether she is in love. But, moving just one step

---

[16] "Preservation of Innocence," *Zero* (Summer, 1949), pp. 18–19.
[17] *Nobody Knows My Name* (New York, 1961), p. 161.
[18] *Ibid.,* p. 162.
[19] *Giovanni's Room* (New York, 1956), p. 12.

ahead of the predatory homosexual underworld, Giovanni's life
demands David's love as its only hope for transcendence. Irrespon-
sibly, and in a way that denies their complexity as human beings,
David disappoints the hopes of Giovanni and disillusions Hella.

What Baldwin registers well is the desperate need for love that
brings transcendence. The homosexual's problem is shown to be the
threat of being forced into the underworld where bought love of
the body, without transcendence, is simply productive of desperation. The women pictured face a similar problem on a heterosexual
level. The world portrayed is nightmarish, but hardly, in any sense,
really vital. One of its serious problems though is that the reader is
not allowed to escape the feeling, in the bad sense, of staginess and
theatricality. The characters are in hell all right, but the reader
never is, and I do not think that this is so simply because the approach to sex is unconventional. The characters do not root themselves deeply enough to become momentous in fictional terms, nor
do they stand with intensity for elemental forces which we are forced
to consider an inescapable part of our lives. So that, despite claims
for complexity, the characters are too easily defined with relationship to a thesis.

Before coming to a consideration of *Another Country,* I should
point out that Baldwin is the author of several stories of distinction, though there is hardly space for more than a brief mentioning
of them. "Previous Condition" is the intense story of a young Negro's attempt to secure his being from its alienated condition within
and the forces of prejudice without. It appeared in *Commentary,*
October, 1948, as Baldwin's first story. "The Death of the Prophet,"
Commentary, March, 1950, was mentioned in connection with *Go
Tell It on the Mountain.* "Come Out the Wilderness " *Mademoi-
selle,* March, 1958, reprinted in *Best Short Stories from Mademoi-
selle,* New York, 1961, explores the lostness of a Negro girl who has
been alienated from her original racial environment. "Sonny's
Blues," *Partisan Review,* Summer, 1957, reprinted in *Best Short
Stories of 1958* and Herbert Gold's *Fiction of the Fifties,* New York,
1959, carries the venture of a Negro boy through narcotics to music
where he finally gains a sense of identity expressed. "This Morning,
This Evening, So Soon," *The Atlantic Monthly,* September, 1960,
reprinted in Martha Foley, *The Best Stories of 1961,* New York,
1961, an issue dedicated to Baldwin, explores the necessity of a successful young Negro actor to come to terms with his place in his-

tory. Each story shows a sure sense of the short story form, a moment of illumination that has significance for the total life of the character. Baldwin's greatest indebtedness in the short story is to Henry James.

Another Country, New York, 1962, Baldwin's latest novel, is a serious and ambitious attempt, a fact which should be recognized despite the fact that to make it a serious novel of the first rank would demand severe cutting and some intensive re-writing. The problem is still that of arriving at a definition of one's being which will be adequately sustaining in the face of the evils of life, and to support another's complexity through love. Both heterosexual and homosexual scenes abound, but, as stated in the discussion of *Giovanni's Room,* these are the instruments for the exploration of being, the metaphors for self-definition and for responsibly entering the complexity of another. They have, therefore, a serious purpose, and Baldwin is too concerned about whether the sex experience provides a transcending love to make distinctions between the heterosexual and homosexual experience. Most of the men have engaged in a homosexual act, and have from it defined their sex for the future; that is, they decide whether the homosexual experience is or is not for their being, with most deciding in favor of heterosexuality.

The first story is that of Rufus, the Negro musician, who is fighting within himself both the real and the imaginary aspects of the race problem, and therefore cannot communicate with Leona, the Southern poor white girl that he picks up with the conscious purpose of sexual exploitation and of getting rid of her before she can "bug" him with her story (i.e., involve him in her complexity as a person). Rufus has suffered real racial persecution, so that even harmless remarks by Leona send him into a rage, and he finally drives her into a nervous breakdown and succumbs to his own frustrations by committing suicide. The horror of their experience is communicated with considerable skill. Rufus's failure in *being* is then re-tested in the lives of other characters who were, in varying degrees, associated with him.

Vivaldo Moore, the Irish-Italian, attracted to Rufus's sister, at first, partly through being a "liberal," and partly because of his sense of having failed her brother, must be made to confront her as a complex human conundrum, capable of ruthless exploitation and high level prostitution: that is, he must lose his innocence.

Cass and Richard Silenski must abandon their oversimplified classifications of each other and achieve a sense of reality in their marriage. Eric, the homosexual, must overthrow his Southern background and come to terms with himself in France. Everybody,
indeed, must learn his own name. Thus the lives of successive sets
of people must come against the problems of being, love, and involvement.

One trouble with the scheme is that so few of the characters ex-
emplify the complexity contended for them. Rufus, Ida, and Eric
are the more adequately developed characters. The rest are not
projected far enough beyond the level of nice, erring people. Thus
the central problem of the book lacks momentousness. Ralph Ellison has said of the novel that ". . . it operates by amplifying and
giving resonance to a specific complex of experience until, through
the eloquence of its statement, that specific part of life speaks metaphorically for the whole." [20] It is precisely the foregoing illusion
that *Another Country* in its totality is unable to create. The section
concerned with the discovery of Rufus's death and the attendance
at his funeral is excessive reportorial detail, sometimes theatrical,
sometimes written at the level of the women's magazine. And the
social criticism is inert, for the most part, a part of the chatty re-
flections of a particular character or of long clinical discussions.

On the other hand, there are some penetrating scenes that reflect
the fine talent of Baldwin. In addition to the story of Rufus, I
should cite most of the scenes where Ida is present and some of the
scenes between Cass Silenski and Eric. In such scenes, the bold use
of naturalistic devices—the sex scenes and four-letter words—project meaning well beyond surface communication. What else could
so well convey Rufus's horrified retching at his dilemma or the terrible exasperation of Ida and Vivaldo? Still, scenes abound in which
naturalistic detail simply thickens the book and the four-letter
words provide a spurious emphasis, galvanizing the reader's attention to no end. And yet *Another Country* is a book that has much
to say, and, as I have tried to indicate, sometimes does.

It is not too much to assert then that Baldwin's novels since *Go
Tell It on the Mountain,* though fine in segments, tend to reflect a
hiatus in his artistic development. In *Go Tell It on the Mountain,*
he was working with a body of understood, crystallized and only par-

20 Granville Hicks, editor, *The Living Novel* (New York, 1957), p. 61.

tially rejected religious and racial mythology that, therefore, carried coiled within it the wires of communication. It is not to say that the artist's challenge and task were simple to point out that he had primarily to manipulate the myth, to steep it in deliberate ambiguity, in order to reflect its Sphinx-like betrayal of those who uncritically absorbed it. The religious interpretation, after all, is within touching distance of the overall idea of Matthew Arnold's famous essay, "Hebraism and Hellenism." His autobiographical intimacy with such material required and received artistic skill and distance. Creating against such a background Baldwin effected a novel which transcended racial and religious categories—became an evoked image of man facing the mysterious universal forces.

On the other hand, the Baldwin of the last two novels confronts the modern consciousness amidst fluxions more talked about than crystallized, and moving at considerable speed: elements of modern man connoting fragmenting certainties eroded at the base, the succor for which has been sought mainly in the vague horizons of the backward look. The workings of sex amidst those fluxions are certainly, in the modern awareness, one major element in the choppy sea of our minds, in which definable shapes seem to appear for the purpose of disappearing. To define them artistically would seem to demand extraordinary effort indeed, whether in traditional or experimental terms.

The conclusion, therefore, to which a full reading of Baldwin seems inescapably to lead is that since his first novel he has not evolved the artistic form that will fully release and articulate his obviously complex awareness. And that to do so may require an abandonment of safety in the use of form equal to that which he has manifested in approach to subject, an act which may concomitantly involve estranging many of the multitude of readers which he has acquired. For an artist of Baldwin's fictional resources, talent, and courage, of his obvious knowledge of evolved fictional techniques, the challenge should hardly be overwhelming.

James Baldwin

by Robert A. Bone

The most important Negro writer to emerge during the last decade is, of course, James Baldwin. His publications, which include three books of essays, three novels, and two plays, have had a stunning impact on our cultural life. His political role as a leading spokesman of the Negro revolt has been scarcely less effective. Awards and honors, wealth and success have crowned his career, and Baldwin has become a national celebrity.

Under the circumstances, the separation of the artist from the celebrity is as difficult as it is necessary. For Baldwin is an uneven writer, the quality of whose work can by no means be taken for granted. His achievement in the novel is most open to dispute, and it is that which I propose to discuss in some detail. Meanwhile, it may be possible to narrow the area of controversy by a preliminary assessment of his talent.

I find Baldwin strongest as an essayist, weakest as a playwright, and successful in the novel form on only one occasion. For the three books of essays, *Notes of a Native Son* (1955), *Nobody Knows My Name* (1961), and *The Fire Next Time* (1963), I have nothing but admiration. Baldwin has succeeded in transposing the entire discussion of American race relations from statistics and sociology to the interior plane; it is a major breakthrough for the American imagination. In the theater, he has written one competent apprentice play, *The Amen Corner,* first produced at Howard University in 1955, and one unspeakably bad propaganda piece, *Blues for Mister Charlie* (1964). In the novel, the impressive achievement of *Go Tell It on the Mountain* (1953) has not been matched by his more recent books, *Giovanni's Room* (1956) and *Another Country* (1962).

Perhaps a closer acquaintance with the author's life will help us to account for this unevenness.

James Baldwin was a product of the Great Migration. His father had come North from New Orleans; his mother, from Maryland. James was born in Harlem in 1924, the first of nine children. His father was a factory worker and lay preacher, and the boy was raised under the twin disciplines of poverty and the store-front church. He experienced a profound religious crisis during the summer of his fourteenth year, entered upon a youthful ministry, and remained in the pulpit for three years. The second crisis of his life was his break with this milieu; that is, with his father's values, hopes, and aspirations for his son. These two crises—the turn into the fold and the turn away—provide the raw material for his first novel and his first play.

Baldwin graduated from De Witt Clinton High School in 1942, having served on the staff of the literary magazine. He had already discovered in this brief encounter a means of transcending his appointed destiny. Shortly after graduation he left home, determined to support himself as best he could while developing his talent as a writer. After six years of frustration and false starts, however, he had two fellowships but no substantial publications to his credit. This initial literary failure, coupled with the pressures of his personal life, drove him into exile. In 1948, at the age of twenty-four, Baldwin left America for Paris, intending never to return.

He remained abroad for nine years. Europe gave him many things. It gave him a world perspective from which to approach the question of his own identity. It gave him a tender love affair, which would dominate the pages of his later fiction. But above all, Europe gave him back himself. Some two years after his arrival in Paris, Baldwin suffered a breakdown and went off to Switzerland to recover:

> There, in that absolutely alabaster landscape, armed with two Bessie Smith records and a typewriter, I began to try to re-create the life that I had first known as a child and from which I had spent so many years in flight. . . . I had never listened to Bessie Smith in America (in the same way that, for years, I would not touch watermelon), but in Europe she helped to reconcile me to being a "nigger." [1]

1 *Nobody Knows My Name* (New York, Dial Press, 1961), p. 5.

The immediate fruit of self-recovery was a great creative outburst. First came two books of reconciliation with his racial heritage. *Go Tell It on the Mountain* and *The Amen Corner* represent a search for roots, a surrender to tradition, an acceptance of the Negro past. Then came a series of essays which probe, deeper than anyone has dared, the psychic history of America. They are a moving record of a man's struggle to define the forces that have shaped him, in order that he may accept himself. Last came *Giovanni's Room,* which explores the question of his male identity. Here Baldwin extends the theme of self-acceptance into the sexual realm.

Toward the end of his stay in Paris, Baldwin experienced the first symptoms of a crisis from which he has never recovered. Having exhausted the theme of self-acceptance, he cast about for fresh material, but his third novel stubbornly refused to move. He has described this moment of panic in a later essay: "It is the point at which many artists lose their minds, or commit suicide, or throw themselves into good works, or try to enter politics." [2] Recognizing these dangers to his art has not enabled Baldwin to avoid them. Something like good works and politics have been the recent bent of his career. Unable to grow as an artist, he has fallen back upon a tradition of protest writing which he formerly denounced.

Baldwin returned to America in 1957. The battered self, he must have felt, was ready to confront society. A good many of the essays in *Nobody Knows My Name* record his initial impressions of America, but this is a transitional book, still largely concerned with questions of identity. Protest, however, becomes the dominant theme of his next three books. In *Another Country, The Fire Next Time,* and *Blues for Mister Charlie,* he assumes the role of Old Testament prophet, calling down the wrath of history on the heads of the white oppressor.

Baldwin's career may be divided into two distinct periods. His first five books have been concerned with the emotion of shame. The flight from self, the quest for identity, and the sophisticated acceptance of one's "blackness" are the themes that flow from this emotion. His last three books have been concerned with the emotion of rage. An apocalyptic vision and a new stridency of tone are brought to bear against the racial and the sexual oppressor. The question then arises, why has he avoided the prophetic role until the recent past?

2 *Ibid.,* p. 224.

The answer, I believe, lies in Baldwin's relationship to his father and, still more, to his spiritual father, Richard Wright. Baldwin's father died in 1943, and within a year Baldwin met Wright for the first time. It is amply clear from his essays that the twenty-year-old youth adopted the older man as a father figure. What followed is simplicity itself: Baldwin's habit of defining himself in opposition to his father was transferred to the new relationship. If Wright was committed to protest fiction, Baldwin would launch his own career with a rebellious essay called "Everybody's Protest Novel." [3] So long as Wright remained alive, the prophetic strain in Baldwin was suppressed. But with Wright's death in 1960, Baldwin was free to *become* his father. He has been giving Noah the rainbow sign ever since.

Go Tell It on the Mountain

The best of Baldwin's novels is *Go Tell It on the Mountain* (1953), and his best is very good indeed. It ranks with Jean Toomer's *Cane,* Richard Wright's *Native Son,* and Ralph Ellison's *Invisible Man* as a major contribution to American fiction. For this novel cuts through the walls of the store-front church to the essence of Negro experience in America. This is Baldwin's earliest world, his bright and morning star, and it glows with metaphorical intensity. Its emotions are his emotions; its language, his native tongue. The result is a prose of unusual power and authority. One senses in Baldwin's first novel a confidence, control, and mastery of style that he has not attained again in the novel form.

The central event of *Go Tell It on the Mountain* is the religious conversion of an adolescent boy. In a long autobiographical essay, which forms a part of *The Fire Next Time,*[4] Baldwin leaves no doubt that he was writing of his own experience. During the summer of his fourteenth year, he tells us, he succumbed to the spiritual seduction of a woman evangelist. On the night of his conversion, he suddenly found himself lying on the floor before the altar. He describes his trancelike state, the singing and clapping of the saints, and the all-night prayer vigil which helped to bring him "through." He then recalls the circumstances of his life that prompted so pagan and desperate a journey to the throne of Grace.

[3] See *Notes of a Native Son* (Boston, Beacon Press, 1955), p. 13–23.
[4] *The Fire Next Time* (New York, Dial Press, 1963), p. 29–61.

The overwhelming fact of Baldwin's childhood was his victimization by the white power structure. At first he experienced white power only indirectly, as refracted through the brutality and degradation of the Harlem ghetto. The world beyond the ghetto seemed remote, and scarcely could be linked in a child's imagination to the harrowing conditions of his daily life. And yet a vague terror, transmitted through his parents to the ghetto child, attested to the power of the white world. Meanwhile, in the forefront of his consciousness was a set of fears by no means vague.

To a young boy growing up in the Harlem ghetto, damnation was a clear and present danger: "For the wages of sin were visible everywhere, in every wine-stained and urine-splashed hallway, in every clanging ambulance bell, in every scar on the faces of the pimps and their whores, in every helpless, newborn baby being brought into this danger, in every knife and pistol fight on the Avenue." [5] To such a boy, the store-front church offered a refuge and a sanctuary from the terrors of the street. God and safety became synonymous, and the church, a part of his survival strategy.

Fear, then, was the principal motive of Baldwin's conversion: "I became, during my fourteenth year, for the first time in my life afraid—afraid of the evil within me and afraid of the evil without." [6] As the twin pressures of sex and race began to mount, the adolescent boy struck a desperate bargain with God. In exchange for sanctuary, he surrendered his sexuality, and abandoned any aspirations that might bring him into conflict with white power. He was safe, but walled off from the world; saved, but isolated from experience. This, to Baldwin, is the historical betrayal of the Negro Church. In exchange for the power of the Word, the Negro trades away the personal power of his sex and the social power of his people.

Life on these terms was unacceptable to Baldwin; he did not care to settle for less than his potential as a man. If his deepest longings were thwarted in the church, he would pursue them through his art. Sexual and racial freedom thus became his constant theme. And yet, even in breaking with the church, he pays tribute to its power: "In spite of everything, there was in the life I fled a zest and a joy and a capacity for facing and surviving disaster that are very mov-

[5] *Ibid.*, p. 34.
[6] *Ibid.*, p. 30.

ing and very rare." [7] We shall confront, then, in *Go Tell It on the Mountain*, a certain complexity of tone. Baldwin maintains an ironic distance from his material, even as he portrays the spiritual force and emotional appeal of store-front Christianity.

So much for the biographical foundations of the novel. The present action commences on the morning of John Grimes' fourteenth birthday, and before the night is out, he is born again in Christ. Part I, "The Seventh Day," introduces us to the boy and his family, his fears and aspirations, and the Temple of the Fire Baptized that is the center of his life. Part II, "The Prayers of the Saints," contains a series of flashbacks in which we share the inmost thoughts and private histories of his Aunt Florence, his mother Elizabeth, and his putative father, Gabriel. Part III, "The Threshing-Floor," returns us to the present and completes the story of the boy's conversion.

Parts I and III are set in Harlem in the spring of 1935. The action of Part II, however, takes place for the most part down home. Florence, Elizabeth, and Gabriel belong to a transitional generation, born roughly between 1875 and 1900. *Go Tell It on the Mountain* is thus a novel of the Great Migration. It traces the process of secularization that occurred when the Negro left the land for the Northern ghettos. This theme, to be sure, is handled ironically. Baldwin's protagonist "gets religion," but he is too young, too frightened, and too innocent to grasp the implications of his choice.

It is through the lives of the adults that we achieve perspective on the boy's conversion. His Aunt Florence has been brought to the evening prayer meeting by her fear of death. She is dying of cancer, and in her extremity humbles herself before God, asking forgiveness of her sins. These have consisted of a driving ambition and a ruthless hardening of heart. Early in her adult life, she left her dying mother to come North, in hopes of bettering her lot. Later, she drove from her side a husband whom she loved: "It had not been her fault that Frank was the way he was, determined to live and die a common nigger" (p. 92).[8] All her deeper feelings have been sacrificed to a futile striving for "whiteness" and respectability. Now she contemplates the wages of her virtue: an agonizing death in a lonely furnished room.

---

[7] *Ibid.*, p. 55.
[8] All page references are to the Dial Press editions of the novels.

Elizabeth, as she conceives her life, has experienced both the fall and the redemption. Through Richard, she has brought an illegitimate child into the world, but through Gabriel, her error is retrieved. She fell in love with Richard during the last summer of her childhood, and followed him North to Harlem. There they took jobs as chambermaid and elevator boy, hoping to be married soon. Richard is sensitive, intelligent, and determined to educate himself. Late one evening, however, he is arrested and accused of armed robbery. When he protests his innocence, he is beaten savagely by the police. Ultimately he is released, but half hysterical with rage and shame, he commits suicide. Under the impact of this blow, Elizabeth retreats from life. Her subsequent marriage to Gabriel represents safety, timidity, and atonement for her sin.

As Gabriel prays on the night of John's conversion his thoughts revert to the events of his twenty-first year: his own conversion and beginning ministry, his joyless marriage to Deborah, and his brief affair with Esther. Deborah had been raped by white men at the age of sixteen. Thin, ugly, sexless, she is treated by the Negroes as a kind of holy fool. Gabriel, who had been a wild and reckless youth, marries her precisely to mortify the flesh. But he cannot master his desire. He commits adultery with Esther, and, informed that she is pregnant, refuses all emotional support. Esther dies in childbirth, and her son, Royal, who grows to manhood unacknowledged by his father, is killed in a Chicago dive.

Soon after the death of Royal, Deborah dies childless, and Gabriel is left without an heir. When he moves North, however, the Lord sends him a sign in the form of an unwed mother and her fatherless child. He marries Elizabeth and promises to raise Johnny as his own son. In the course of time the second Royal is born, and Gabriel rejoices in the fulfillment of God's promise. But John's half brother, the fruit of the prophet's seed, has turned his back on God. Tonight he lies at home with a knife wound, inflicted in a street fight with some whites. To Gabriel, therefore, John's conversion is a bitter irony: "Only the son of the bondwoman stood where the rightful heir should stand" (p. 128).

Through this allusion, Baldwin alerts us to the metaphorical possibilities of his plot. Gabriel's phrase is from Genesis 21: 9–10, "And Sarah saw the son of Hagar the Egyptian, which she had born unto Abraham, mocking. Wherefore she said unto Abraham, Cast out this bondwoman and her son: for the son of the bondwoman shall not be heir with my son, even with Isaac." Hagar's bastard son is of course Ishmael, the archetypal outcast. Apparently Baldwin wants us to view Gabriel and Johnny in metaphorical relation to Abraham and Ishmael. This tableau of guilty father and rejected son will serve him as an emblem of race relations in America.

Baldwin sees the Negro quite literally as the bastard child of American civilization. In Gabriel's double involvement with bastardy we have a re-enactment of the white man's historic crime. In Johnny, the innocent victim of Gabriel's hatred, we have an archetypal image of the Negro child. Obliquely, by means of an extended metaphor, Baldwin approaches the very essence of Negro experience. That essence is rejection, and its most destructive consequence is shame. But God, the Heavenly Father, does not reject the Negro utterly. He casts down only to raise up. This is the psychic drama that occurs beneath the surface of John's conversion.

The Negro child, rejected by the whites for reasons that he cannot understand, is afflicted by an overwhelming sense of shame. Something mysterious, he feels, must be wrong with him, that he should be so cruelly ostracized. In time he comes to associate these feelings with the color of his skin—the basis, after all, of his rejection. He feels, and is made to feel, perpetually dirty and unclean:

> John hated sweeping this carpet, for dust arose, clogging his nose and sticking to his sweaty skin, and he felt that should he sweep it forever, the clouds of dust would not diminish, the rug would not be clean. It became in his imagination his impossible, lifelong task, his hard trial, like that of a man he had read about somewhere, whose curse it was to push a boulder up a steep hill. [p. 27]

This quality of Negro life, unending struggle with one's own blackness, is symbolized by Baldwin in the family name, Grimes. One can readily understand how such a sense of personal shame might have been inflamed by contact with the Christian tradition and transformed into an obsession with original sin. Gabriel's sermons take off from such texts as "I am a man of unclean lips," or "He which is filthy, let him be filthy still." The Negro's religious ritual, as Baldwin points out in an early essay, is permeated with color symbolism: "Wash me, cried the slave to his Maker, and I

shall be whiter, whiter than snow! For black is the color of evil;
only the robes of the saved are white." [9]

Given this attack on the core of the self, how can the Negro respond? If he accepts the white man's equation of blackness with
evil, he is lost. Hating his true self, he will undertake the construc-
tion of a counter-self along the line that everything "black" he now
disowns. To such a man, Christ is a kind of spiritual bleaching
cream. Only if the Negro challenges the white man's moral categories can he hope to survive on honorable terms. This involves
the sentiment that everything "black" he now embraces, however
painfully, as his. There is, in short, the path of self-hatred and the
path of self-acceptance. Both are available to Johnny within the
framework of the Church, but he is deterred from one by the negative example of his father.

Consider Gabriel. The substance of his life is moral evasion. A
preacher of the gospel and secretly the father of an illegitimate
child, he cannot face the evil in himself. In order to preserve his
image as the Lord's anointed, he has sacrificed the lives of those
around him. His principal victim is Johnny, who is not his natural
child. In disowning the bastard, he disowns the "blackness" in
himself. Gabriel's psychological mechanisms are, so to say, white.
Throughout his work Baldwin has described the scapegoat mech-
anism that is fundamental to the white man's sense of self. To the
question, Who am I?, the white man answers: I am *white,* that is
immaculate, without stain. I am the purified, the saved, the saintly,
the elect. It is the *black* who is the embodiment of evil. Let him,
the son of the bondwoman, pay the price of my sins.

From self-hatred flows not only self-righteousness but self-glori-
fication as well. From the time of his conversion Gabriel has been
living in a world of compensatory fantasy. He sees the Negro race
as a chosen people and himself as prophet and founder of a royal
line. But if Old Testament materials can be appropriated to but-
tress such a fantasy world, they also offer a powerful means of grappling with reality. When the Negro preacher compares the lot of
his people to that of the children of Israel, he provides his flock
with a series of metaphors corresponding to their deepest experience. The Church thus offers to the Negro masses a ritual enactment
of their daily pain. It is with this poetry of suffering, which Baldwin

9 *Notes of a Native Son,* p. 21.

calls the power of the Word, that the final section of the novel is concerned.

The first fifteen pages of Part III contain some of Baldwin's most effective writing. As John Grimes lies before the altar, a series of visionary states passes through his soul. Dream fragments and Freudian sequences, lively fantasies and Aesopian allegories, combine to produce a generally surrealistic effect. Images of darkness and chaos, silence and emptiness, mist and cold—cumulative patterns developed early in the novel—function now at maximum intensity. These images of damnation express the state of the soul when thrust into outer darkness by a rejecting, punishing, castrating father figure who is the surrogate of a hostile society. The dominant emotions are shame, despair, guilt, and fear.

At the depth of John's despair, a sound emerges to assuage his pain:

> He had heard it all his life, but it was only now that his ears were opened to this sound that came from the darkness, that could only come from darkness, that yet bore such sure witness to the glory of the light. And now in his moaning, and so far from any help, he heard it in himself—it rose from his bleeding, his cracked-open heart. It was a sound of rage and weeping which filled the grave, rage and weeping from time set free, but bound now in eternity; rage that had no language, weeping with no voice—which yet spoke now, to John's startled soul, of boundless melancholy, of the bitterest patience, and the longest night; of the deepest water, the strongest chains, the most cruel lash; of humility most wretched, the dungeon most absolute, of love's bed defiled, and birth dishonored, and most bloody, unspeakable, sudden death. Yes, the darkness hummed with murder: the body in the water, the body in the fire, the body on the tree. John looked down the line of these armies of darkness, army upon army, and his soul whispered, *Who are these?* [p. 228]

This is the sound, though John Grimes doesn't know it, of the blues. It is the sound of Bessie Smith, to which James Baldwin listened as he wrote *Go Tell It on the Mountain.* It is the sound of all Negro art and all Negro religion, for it flows from the cracked-open heart.

On these harsh terms, Baldwin's protagonist discovers his identity. He belongs to those armies of darkness and must forever share their pain. To the question, Who am I? he can now reply: I am he who suffers, and yet whose suffering on occasion is "from time set

free." And thereby he discovers his humanity, for only man can rit-
ualize his pain. We are now very close to that plane of human experience where art and religion intersect. What Baldwin wants us
to feel is the emotional pressure exerted on the Negro's cultural
forms by his exposure to white oppression. And finally to comprehend that these forms alone, through their power of transforming
suffering, have enabled him to survive his terrible ordeal.

Giovanni's Room

Giovanni's Room (1956) is by far the weakest of Baldwin's novels. There is a tentative, unfinished quality about the book, as if in
merely broaching the subject of homosexuality Baldwin had exhausted his creative energy. Viewed in retrospect, it seems less a
novel in its own right than a first draft of *Another Country*. The
surface of the novel is deliberately opaque, for Baldwin is struggling
to articulate the most intimate, the most painful, the most elusive
of emotions. The characters are vague and disembodied, the themes
half-digested, the colors rather bleached than vivified. We recognize
in this sterile psychic landscape the unprocessed raw material of art.

And yet this novel occupies a key position in Baldwin's spiritual
development. Links run backward to *Go Tell It on the Mountain*
as well as forward to *Another Country*. The very furniture of Baldwin's mind derives from the store-front church of his boyhood and
adolescence. When he attempts a novel of homosexual love, with
an all-white cast of characters and a European setting, he simply
transposes the moral topography of Harlem to the streets of Paris.
When he strives toward sexual self-acceptance he automatically casts
the homosexual in a priestly role.

Before supporting this interpretation, let me summarize the plot.
David, an American youth living abroad in Paris, meets a girl from
back home and asks her to marry him. Hella is undecided, however,
and she goes to Spain to think it over. During her absence, David
meets Giovanni, a proud and handsome young Italian. They fall
deeply in love and have a passionate affair. When Hella returns,
David is forced to choose between his male lover and his American
fiancée. He abandons Giovanni to the homosexual underworld,
which is only too eager to claim him. When Guillaume, whom
Baldwin describes as "a disgusting old fairy," inflicts upon the
youth a series of humiliations, Giovanni strangles his tormentor.

He is tried for murder and executed by the guillotine. Meanwhile David, who has gone with Hella to the south of France, cannot forget Giovanni. Tortured by guilt and self-doubt, he breaks off his engagement by revealing the truth about himself.

At the emotional center of the novel is the relationship between David and Giovanni. It is highly symbolic, and to understand what is at stake, we must turn to Baldwin's essay on André Gide.[10] Published toward the end of 1954, about a year before the appearance of *Giovanni's Room*, this essay is concerned with the two sides of Gide's personality and the precarious balance that was struck between them. On the one side was his sensuality, his lust for the boys on the Piazza d'Espagne, threatening him always with utter degradation. On the other was his Protestantism, his purity, his otherworldliness—that part of him which was not carnal, and which found expression in his Platonic marriage to Madeleine. As Baldwin puts it, "She was his Heaven who would forgive him for his Hell and help him to endure it." It is a drama of salvation, in which the celibate wife, through selfless dedication to the suffering artist, becomes in effect a priest.

In the novel Giovanni plays the role of Gide; David, of Madeleine. Giovanni is not merely a sensualist, but a Platonist as well: "I want to escape . . . this dirty world, this dirty body" (p. 35). It is the purity of Giovanni's love for David—its idealized, transcendent quality—that protects him from a kind of homosexual Hell. David is the string connecting him to Heaven, and when David abandons him, he plunges into the abyss.

We can now appreciate the force of David's remark, "The burden of his salvation seemed to be on me and I could not endure it" (p. 168). Possessing the power to save, David rejects the priestly office. Seen in this light, his love affair with Giovanni is a kind of novitiate. The dramatic conflict of the novel can be stated as follows: does David have a true vocation? Is he prepared to renounce the heterosexual world? When David leaves Giovanni for Hella, he betrays his calling, but ironically he has been ruined for both the priesthood and the world.

It is Giovanni, Baldwin's doomed hero, who is the true priest. For a priest is nothing but a journeyman in suffering. Thus Giovanni defies David, the American tourist, even to understand his

10 See *Nobody Knows My Name*, p. 155–62.

village: "And you will have no idea of the life there, dripping and bursting and beautiful and terrible, as you have no idea of my life now" (p. 203). It is a crucial distinction for all of Baldwin's work: there are the relatively innocent—the *laity* who are mere apprentices in human suffering—and the fully initiated, the *clergy* who are intimate with pain. Among the laity may be numbered Americans, white folks, heterosexuals, and squares; among the clergy, Europeans, Negroes, homosexuals, hipsters, and jazzmen. The finest statement of this theme, in which the jazzman is portrayed as priest, is Baldwin's moving story, "Sonny's Blues." [11]

Assumption of the priestly role is always preceded by an extraordinary experience of suffering, often symbolized in Baldwin's work by the death of a child. Thus in *The Amen Corner* Sister Margaret becomes a store-front church evangelist after giving birth to a dead child. And in *Giovanni's Room* the protagonist leaves his wife, his family, and his village after the birth of a stillborn child: "When I knew that it was dead I took our crucifix off the wall and I spat on it and I threw it on the floor and my mother and my girl screamed and I went out" (p. 205). It is at this point that Giovanni's inverted priesthood begins. Like Gide, he rebels against God, but the priestly impulse persists. He retreats from the heterosexual world, achieves a kind of purity in his relationship with David, is betrayed, and is consigned to martyrdom.

The patterns first explored in *Giovanni's Room* are given full expression in *Another Country*. Rufus is a Negro Giovanni—a journeyman in suffering and a martyr to racial oppression. Vivaldo and the other whites are mere apprentices, who cannot grasp the beauty and the terror of Negro life. Eric is a David who completes his novitiate, and whose priestly or redemptive role is central to the novel. There has been, however, a crucial change of tone. In *Giovanni's Room* one part of Baldwin wants David to escape from the male prison, even as another part remains committed to the ideal of homosexual love. In the later novel, this conflict has been resolved. Baldwin seems convinced that homosexuality is a liberating force, and he now brings to the·subject a certain proselytizing zeal.

11 See *Partisan Review* (summer 1957), p. 327–58.

Another Country

Another Country (1962) is a failure on the grand scale. It is an ambitious novel, rich in thematic possibilities, for Baldwin has at his disposal a body of ideas brilliantly developed in his essays. When he tries to endow these ideas with imaginative life, however, his powers of invention are not equal to the task. The plot consists of little more than a series of occasions for talk and fornication. Since the latter is a limited vehicle for the expression of complex ideas, talk takes over, and the novel drowns in a torrent of rhetoric.

The ideas themselves are impressive enough. At the heart of what Baldwin calls the white problem is a moral cowardice, a refusal to confront the "dark" side of human experience. The white American, at once overprotected and repressed, exhibits an infuriating tendency to deny the reality of pain and suffering, violence and evil, sex and death. He preserves in the teeth of human circumstance what must strike the less protected as a kind of willful innocence.

The American Negro, exposed to the ravages of reality by his status as a slave, has never enjoyed the luxury of innocence. On the contrary, his dark skin has come to be associated, at some buried level of the white psyche, with those forbidden impulses and hidden terrors which the white man is afraid to face. The unremitting daily warfare of American race relations must be understood in these symbolic terms. By projecting the "blackness" of his own being upon the dark skin of his Negro victim, the white man hopes to exorcise the chaotic forces that threaten to destroy him from within.

The psychic cost is of course enormous. The white man loses the experience of "blackness," sacrificing both its beauty and its terror to the illusion of security. In the end, he loses his identity. For a man who cannot acknowledge the dark impulses of his own soul cannot have the vaguest notion of who he is. A stranger to himself and others, the most salient feature of his personality will be a fatal bewilderment.

There are psychic casualties on the Negro side as well. No human personality can escape the effects of prolonged emotional rejection. The victim of this cruelty will defend himself with hatred and with dreams of vengeance, and will lose, perhaps forever, his normal capacity for love. Strictly speaking, this set of defenses, and the threat of self-destruction which they pose, constitutes the Negro problem.

It is up to the whites to break this vicious circle of rejection and hatred. They can do so only by facing the void, by confronting chaos, by making the necessary journey to "another country." What the white folks need is a closer acquaintance with the blues. Then perhaps they will be ready to join the human race. But only if the bloodless learn to bleed will it be possible for the Negro to lay down his burden of hatred and revenge.

So much for the conceptual framework of the novel. What dramatic materials are employed to invest these themes with life? A Greenwich Village setting and a hipster idiom ("Beer, dad, then we'll split"). A square thrown in for laughs. A good deal of boozing, and an occasional stick of tea. Some male cheesecake ("He bent down to lift off the scarlet bikini"). Five orgasms (two interracial and two homosexual) or approximately one per eighty pages, a significant increase over the Mailer rate. Distracted by this nonsense, how can one attend to the serious business of the novel?

In one respect only does the setting of *Another Country* succeed. Baldwin's descriptions of New York contain striking images of malaise, scenes and gestures that expose the moral chaos of contemporary urban life. The surface of his prose reflects the aching loneliness of the city with the poignancy of a Hopper painting. Harassed commuters and jostled pedestrians seem to yearn for closer contact. Denizens of a Village bar clutch their drinks with a gesture of buried despair. The whir of cash registers and the blatant glare of neon signs proclaim the harsh ascendancy of the commercial spirit. The tense subway crowds and the ubiquitous police convey a sense of latent violence. The furtive scribblings on lavatory walls provide a chilling commentary, in their mixture of raw lust and ethnic hate, on the scope and depth of our depravity.

Structurally speaking, the novel consists of two articulating parts. Book I is concerned to demonstrate how bad things really are in this America. Books II and III encompass the redemptive movement, the symbolic journey to "another country."

The central figure of Book I is Rufus Scott, a talented jazz drummer who is driven to suicide by the pressures of a racist society. Sensitive, bitter, violent, he sublimates his hatred by pounding on the white skin of his drums. With something of the same malice, he torments his white mistress, ultimately driving her insane.

Crushed by this burden of guilt, he throws himself from the George Washington Bridge. Rufus, in short, is a peculiarly passive Bigger Thomas, whose murderous impulses turn back upon himself. Like Bigger, he was created to stir the conscience of the nation. For the underlying cause of Rufus' death is the failure of his white friends to comprehend the depth of his despair.

In the melting pot of Greenwich Village, Baldwin brings together a group of white Americans whose lives are linked to Rufus' fate. Rufus' closest friend is Vivaldo Moore, an "Irish wop" who has escaped from the slums of Brooklyn. Cass, a girl of upperclass New England stock, has rebelled against her background to marry an aspiring writer. Eric Jones, having left Alabama for an acting career in New York, has experienced a double exile, and is about to return from a two-year sojourn in France.

Each of these friends has failed Rufus in his hour of need. It is the moral obtuseness of the whites that Baldwin means to stress. Rufus stands in relation to his friends as jazzman to audience: "Now he stood before the misty doors of the jazz joint, peering in, sensing rather than seeing the *frantic* black people on the stand and the *oblivious,* mixed crowd at the bar" (pp. 4–5, my emphasis). The audience simply refuses to hear the frantic plea in an insistent riff which seems to ask, "Do you love me?" It is a failure of love, but still more of imagination. Vivaldo and the others fail to transcend their innocence. They are blinded by their fear of self. Meaning well, they acquiesce in Rufus' death.

Having killed off Rufus early in the novel, Baldwin pursues the theme of vengeance and reconciliation through the character of Ida Scott. Embittered by the death of her brother, on whom she had counted to save her from the streets of Harlem, Ida takes revenge on the nearest white man. She moves in with Vivaldo, ostensibly in love, but actually exploiting the arrangement to advance her career as a blues singer. Toward the end of the novel, however, Vivaldo achieves a new sense of reality. This enables Ida, who has come reluctantly to love him, to confess to her deception. In a gesture of reconciliation, she slips from her finger a ruby-eyed snake ring—a gift from Rufus, and a symbol of her heritage of hate.

Books II and III are dominated by the figure of Eric Jones, the young actor who has gone abroad to find himself. His adolescence in Alabama was marked by a homosexual encounter with a Negro youth. In New York he has a brief, violent, and radically unsatisfying affair with Rufus, from which he flees to France. There he falls in love with Yves, a Paris street boy, and through a chaste and tactful courtship wins his trust and love. As Book II opens, they are enjoying an idyllic holiday in a rented villa on the Côte d'Azur. Eric must soon leave for America, however, where he has accepted a part in a Broadway play. After a suitable interval, Yves will join him in New York.

Since the love affair of Eric and Yves is the turning point of the novel, we must pause to examine its wider implications. Book II commences with highly charged, symbolic prose:

> Eric sat naked in his rented garden. Flies buzzed and boomed in the brilliant heat, and a yellow bee circled his head. Eric remained very still, then reached for the cigarettes beside him and lit one, hoping that the smoke would drive the bee away. Yves' tiny black-and-white kitten stalked the garden as though it were Africa, crouching beneath the mimosas like a panther and leaping into the air. [p. 183]

Like Whitman, his spiritual progenitor, Baldwin tends to endow his diffuse sexuality with mythic significance. Here he depicts, in this Mediterranean garden, what appears to be a homosexual Eden. Then, in an attempt to fuse two levels of his own experience, he brings into metaphorical relation the idea of homosexuality and the idea of Africa. Each represents to the "majority" imagination a kind of primal chaos, yet each contains the possibility of liberation. For to be Negro, or to be homosexual, is to be in constant touch with that sensual reality which the white (read: heterosexual) world is at such pains to deny.

The male lovers, naked in the garden, are not to be taken too literally. What Baldwin means to convey through this idyllic episode is the innocence of the unrepressed. He has been reading, one would surmise, Norman Brown's *Life against Death*. "Children," Brown reminds us, "explore in indiscriminate fashion all the erotic potentialities of the human body. In Freudian terms, children are polymorphously perverse." [12] In this episode on the Mediterranean coast we are back in the cradle of man, back in the sexually and racially undifferentiated human past; back in the lost paradise of the polymorphously perverse.

On these mythic foundations, Baldwin constructs a theory of personality. The primal stuff of human personality is undifferen-

12 Norman Brown, *Life against Death* (Wesleyan University Press, 1959), p. 27.

tiated: "He was, briefly and horribly, in a region where there were no definitions of any kind, neither of color nor of male and female" (pp. 301–2). One must face this formlessness, however, before one can hope to achieve form.

At the core of Baldwin's fiction is an existentialist psychology. In a passage whose language is reminiscent of Genesis, he describes Vivaldo's struggle to define himself: "And beneath all this was the void where anguish lived and questions crouched, which referred only to Vivaldo and to no one else on earth. Down there, down there, lived the raw unformed substance for the creation of Vivaldo, and only he, Vivaldo alone, could master it" (pp. 305–6). As music depends ultimately on silence, so being is achieved in tension with nothingness. Sexual identity—all identity—emerges from the void. Man, the sole creator of himself, moves alone upon the face of the waters.

We can now account for Eric's pivotal position in the novel. Through his commitment to Yves, he introduces an element of order into the chaos of his personal life. This precarious victory, wrested in anguish from the heart of darkness, is the real subject of *Another Country*. Images of chaos proliferate throughout the novel. Rufus leaps into chaos when he buries himself in the deep black water of the Hudson River. Cass encounters chaos in the strange, pulsating life of Harlem, or in an abstract expressionist canvas at the Museum of Modern Art. To Vivaldo, chaos means a marijuana party in a Village pad; to Eric, the male demimonde that threatens to engulf him. Eric is the first of Rufus' friends to face his demons and achieve a sense of self. He in turn emancipates the rest.

From this vantage point, one can envision the novel that Baldwin was trying to write. With the breakdown of traditional standards—even of sexual normality—homosexuality becomes a metaphor of the modern condition. Baldwin says of Eric, "There were no standards for him except those he could make for himself" (p. 212). Forced to create his own values as he goes along, Eric is to serve "as a footnote to the twentieth century torment" (p. 330). The homosexual becomes emblematic of existential man.

What actually happens, however, is that Baldwin's literary aims are deflected by his sexual mystique. Eric returns to America as the high priest of ineffable phallic mysteries. His friends, male and female, dance around the Maypole and, *mirabile dictu*, their sense of reality is restored. Cass commits adultery with Eric, and is thereby reconciled to her faltering marriage. Vivaldo receives at Eric's hands a rectal revelation that prepares him for the bitter truth of Ida's confession. The novel ends as Yves joins Eric in New York, heralding, presumably, a fresh start for all and a new era of sexual and racial freedom.

For most readers of *Another Country,* the difficulty will lie in accepting Eric as a touchstone of reality. Let us consider the overall design. Rufus is portrayed as the victim of a white society that cannot face unpleasant truths. The redemptive role is then assigned to Eric. But few will concede a sense of reality, at least in the sexual realm, to one who regards heterosexual love as "a kind of superior calisthenics" (p. 336). To most, homosexuality will seem rather an evasion than an affirmation of human truth. Ostensibly the novel summons us to reality. Actually it substitutes for the illusions of white supremacy those of homosexual love.

In any event, it is the task of a literary critic not to debate the merits of homosexuality but to demonstrate its pressure on the novel. Let us accept Baldwin's postulate that in order to become a man, one must journey to the void. Let us grant that homosexuality is a valid metaphor of this experience. We must now ask of Baldwin's hero: does he face the void and emerge with a new sense of reality, or does he pitch his nomad's tent forever on the shores of the burning lake? The answer hinges, it seems to me, on the strength of Eric's commitment to Yves. Baldwin describes it as total, and yet, within a few weeks' span, while Yves remains behind in France, Eric betrays him with a woman and a man. How can we grant to this lost youth redemptive power?

One senses that Baldwin, in his portrait of Eric, has desired above all to be faithful to his own experience. He will neither falsify nor go beyond it. Central to that experience is a rebellion against the prevailing sexual, as well as racial mores. But on either plane of experience, Baldwin faces an emotional dilemma. Like Satan and the fallen angels, it is as painful to persist in his rebellion as to give it up. Total defiance is unthinkable, total reconciliation only less so. These are the poles of Baldwin's psychic life, and the novel vacillates helplessly between them.

The drama of reconciliation is enacted by Ida and Vivaldo. Through their symbolic marriage Ida is reconciled to whites; Vivaldo, to women. This gesture, however, is a mere concession to majority opinion. What Baldwin really feels is dramatized through Rufus and Eric. Rufus can be neither fully reconciled to nor fully defiant of white society. No Bigger Thomas, he is incapable of total hate. Pushed to the limits of endurance, he commits suicide. Similarly, Eric cannot be fully reconciled to women, nor can he surrender to the male demimonde. So he camps on the outskirts of Hell. In the case of Rufus, the suicidal implications are overt. With Eric, as we shall see, Baldwin tries to persuade us that Hell is really Heaven.

In its rhetoric as well, the novel veers between the poles of reconciliation and defiance. At times the butter of brotherhood seems to melt in Baldwin's mouth. But here is Rufus, scoring the first interracial orgasm of the book: "And shortly, nothing could have stopped him, not the white God himself nor a lynch mob arriving on wings. Under his breath he cursed the milk-white bitch and groaned and rode his weapon between her thighs" (p. 22). With what economy of phrase "the milk-white bitch" combines hostility to whites and women! Nowhere is Baldwin's neurotic conflict more nakedly exposed. On one side we have the white God and the lynch mob, determined to suppress sex. On the other, adolescent rebellion and the smashing of taboo, hardening at times into Garveyism.

By Garveyism I mean the emotional and rhetorical excess, and often the extravagant fantasies, to which an embattled minority may resort in promoting its own defense. *Another Country* is doubly susceptible to these temptations, for it was conceived as a joint assault on racial and sexual intolerance. Apparently prejudice encountered in either context will evoke a similar response. The arrogance of the majority has a natural counterpart in exaggerated claims of minority supremacy.

In the racial sphere Baldwin employs defenses that go well beyond a healthy race pride or a legitimate use of folk material. His portrait of Ida, for example, leans heavily on the exotic, on that stereotype of jungle grace which flourished in the 1920s. To a touch of primitivism he adds flat assertions of superiority: Negroes are more alive, more colorful, more spontaneous, better dancers, and, above all, better lovers than the pale, gray, milk-white, chalk-white, dead-white, ice-hearted, frozen-limbed, stiff-assed zombies from downtown. Well, perhaps. One does not challenge the therapeutic value of these pronouncements, only their artistic relevance.

Coupled with these racial sentiments are manifestations of sexual

Garveyism. Throughout the novel the superiority of homosexual love is affirmed. Here alone can one experience total surrender and full orgastic pleasure; here alone, the metaphysical terror of the void. Heterosexual love, by comparison, is a pale—one is tempted to say, white—imitation. In many passages hostility to women reaches savage proportions: "Every time I see a woman wearing her fur coats and her jewels and her gowns, I want to tear all that off her and drag her someplace, to a *pissoir,* and make her smell the smell of many men, the *piss* of many men, and make her know that *that* is what she is for" (p. 210).

It may be argued that these are the sentiments of Yves and not of Baldwin, but that is precisely the point. In *Another Country* the sharp outlines of character are dissolved by waves of uncontrolled emotion. The novel lacks a proper distancing. One has the impression of Baldwin's recent work that the author does not know where his own psychic life leaves off and that of his characters begins. What is more, he scarcely cares to know, for he is sealed in a narcissism so engrossing that he fails to make emotional contact with his characters. If his people have no otherness, if he repeatedly violates their integrity, how can they achieve the individuality which alone will make them memorable?

In conclusion, I should like to view *Another Country* from the perspective of the author's spiritual journey. Reduced to its essentials, this journey has carried Baldwin from a store-front church in Harlem to a Greenwich Village pad. His formative years were spent among the saints, in an environment where repressive attitudes toward sex were paramount. As a result, his sexual experience has always contained a metaphysical dimension, bearing inescapably on his relationship to God. To understand the failure of *Another Country* we must trace the connection between his sexual rebellion, his religious conceptions, and his style.

Baldwin has described the spiritual geography of his adolescence in the opening pages of *The Fire Next Time.* On a little island in the vast sea of Harlem stood the saved, who had fled for their very lives into the Church. All around them was the blazing Hell of the Avenue, with its bars and brothels, pimps and junkies, violence and crime. Between God and the Devil an unrelenting contest was waged for the souls of the young, in which the girls of God's party bore a special burden: "They understood that they must act as God's decoys, saving the souls of the boys for Jesus and binding the bodies of the boys in marriage. For this was the beginning of our burning time." [13]

Baldwin's adolescent rebellion began, it seems plain, when his dawning sensuality collided with his youthful ministry. At first he rebelled against the store-front church, then Harlem, seeking to escape at any cost. Ultimately he came to reject the female sex, the white world, and the Christian God. As his rebellion grew, he discovered in his gift for language a means of liberation. Like hundreds of American writers, he fled from the provinces (in his case, Harlem) to Greenwich Village and the Left Bank. There he hoped to find a haven of sexual, racial, and intellectual freedom.

He quickly discovered, however, that he had not left the Avenue behind. In Greenwich Village or its French equivalent, he peered into the abyss, the demimonde of gay bars, street boys, and male prostitutes. This he recognized as Hell and recoiled in horror. But what alternative does he offer to promiscuity and fleeting physical encounter? He speaks in the rhetoric of commitment and responsibility, but what he has in mind is simply a homosexual version of romantic love. It is a familiar spiritual maneuver. Baldwin has built a palace on the ramparts of Hell and called it Heaven. Its proper name is Pandemonium.

In an effort to make Hell endurable, Baldwin attempts to spiritualize his sexual rebellion. Subjectively, I have no doubt, he is convinced that he has found God. Not the white God of his black father, but a darker deity who dwells in the heart of carnal mystery. One communes with this dark power through what Baldwin calls "the holy and liberating orgasm." [14] The stranger the sex partner, the better the orgasm, for it violates a stronger taboo. Partners of a different race, or the same sex, or preferably both, afford the maximum spiritual opportunities.

Baldwin imagines his new faith to be a complete break with the past, but in fact he has merely inverted the Christian orthodoxy of his youth. Properly regarded, *Another Country* will be seen as the celebration of a Black Mass. The jazzman is Baldwin's priest; the homosexual, his acolyte. The bandstand is his altar; Bessie Smith, his choir. God is carnal mystery, and through orgasm the Word is made flesh. Baldwin's ministry is as vigorous as ever. He summons to the mourners' bench all who remain, so to say, hard-

---

[13] *The Fire Next Time*, p. 32.
[14] See *Blues for Mister Charlie* (New York, Dial Press, 1964), p. 105.

ened in their innocence. Lose that, he proclaims, and you will be saved. To the truly unregenerate, those stubborn heterosexuals, he offers the prospect of salvation through sodomy. With this novel doctrine the process of inversion is complete.

These contentions are best supported by a look at Baldwin's style. Two idioms were available to him from the Negro world: the consecrated and the profane. They derive respectively from the church-oriented and the jazz-oriented segments of the Negro community. To Baldwin the church idiom signifies submission, reconciliation, brotherhood, and platonic love. Conversely, the hipster idiom conveys rebellion, defiance, retaliation, and sexual love.

The predominant mode of *Another Country* is the hipster idiom. For Baldwin it is the language of apostasy. In rejecting the God of his youth, he inverts the consecrated language of the saints. The general effect is blasphemous: "What a pain in the ass Old Jesus Christ has turned out to be, and it probably wasn't even the poor, doomed, loving, hopheaded old Jew's fault" (p. 308). Baldwin's diction is deliberately shocking; its function is to challenge limits, to transgress. In the sexual realm it exploits the fascination of the forbidden, like a cheap film aimed at the teen-age trade. Indeed, if the style proclaims the man, we are dealing with an adolescent: who else gets his kicks from the violation of taboo?

Curiously, however, the language of the store-front church persists. For the hipster idiom is really Baldwin's second language, and in moments of high emotion he reverts to his native tongue. This occurs primarily when he tries to heighten or exalt the moment of sexual union. In the vicinity of orgasm his diction acquires a religious intensity; his metaphors announce the presence of a new divinity: "When he entered that marvelous wound in her, *rending and tearing! rending and tearing!* was he surrendering, in joy, to the Bridegroom, Lord, and Savior?" (p. 308, emphasis in original).

This sudden shift into the church idiom betrays on Baldwin's part a deep need to spiritualize his sexual revolt. Here he describes Eric's first homosexual encounter: "What had always been *hidden* was to him, that day, *revealed,* and it did not matter that, fifteen years later, he sat in an armchair, overlooking a foreign sea, still struggling to find that *grace* which would allow him to bear that *revelation*" (p. 206, emphasis supplied). This is the language of Pandemonium: evil has become Baldwin's good. The loss of meaning that ensues is both moral and semantic, and the writer who permits it betrays both self and craft.

Another Country is not simply a bad novel, but a dead end. It is symptomatic of a severe crisis in Baldwin's life and art. The author's popular acclaim, his current role as a political celebrity, and the Broadway production of his recent play have all tended to obscure the true state of affairs. But Baldwin must suspect that his hipster phase is coming to a close. He has already devoted two novels to his sexual rebellion. If he persists, he will surely be remembered as the greatest American novelist since Jack Kerouac. The future now depends on his ability to transcend the emotional reflexes of his adolescence. So extraordinary a talent requires of him no less an effort.

The Lesson of the Master:
Henry James and James Baldwin

by Charles Newman

> The moral is that the flower of art blooms only where the soil
> is deep, that it takes a great deal of history to produce a little
> literature, that it needs a complex social machinery to set a
> writer in motion.
>
> HENRY JAMES

James Baldwin has made a reputation by exploiting social
paradoxes, so it should not be surprising to trace his literary ante-
cedents to neither Richard Wright nor Harriet B. Stowe, but to
that Brahmin, Henry James. Consider this sentence, for example:

> For what, at bottom, distinguished the Americans from the Negroes
> who surrounded us, men from Nigeria, Barbados, Martinique—so
> many names for so many disciplines—was the banal and quite over-
> whelming fact that we had been born in a society which, in a way
> quite inconceivable for Africans, and no longer real for Europeans,
> was open, and in a sense, which has nothing to do with justice or
> injustice, was free.

The amphibian elegance of such syntax comes naturally to an
artist obsessed by dualities, paradox. The Atlantic Ocean separated
James's mind into opposed hemispheres, and the gulf of color so
cleaves Baldwin. The antipodes of their worlds propose a dialectical
art.

Such patent oppositions often prove disastrous in fiction, insofar
as they tend to oversimplify character and conflict. So, to be fair, it
should be noted at the outset that Baldwin's characters suffer no

more from their color than James's suffer from their money—these are only the peculiar conditions of their suffering. The problem for both is more universal—the opacity of their culture and the question of their identity within it. For Baldwin assumes, in the consequences of his culture, the crisis of his identity, the reflective burden of Western Man. His color is his metaphor, his vantage. But in his despair, he is closer to Henry Adams than John Henry.

Both Baldwin and James were victims of a "mysterious childhood accident." Only their society's different reaction to puberty sets them apart. It is not so much a question of how it happened, but the consequences. "I'm the reaction against the mistake," says Lambert Strether in *The Ambassadors,* and Baldwin certifies this most finally for his contemporaries. "They were so other," James elaborates in *A Small Boy and Others,* "that was what I felt; and to be other, *other almost anyhow,* seemed as good as the probable taste of the bright compound wistfully watched in the confectioner's window" (emphasis mine).

Their hurts are obscure only because such wounds are generally ignored by those enamored of the big candy in the window. The pose necessitated is that of the *powerless, feeling young man.* The psychological consequence is self-imposed exile; to be "other almost anyhow." The literary consequence is the novel of "manners" (read prejudice); this being the drama of how personal histories conflict with the public history of the time. Personal action can only be understood in terms of its public consequences. Morality, in this sense, may not be relative, but it is always comparative.

The two exiles share a further insight. Both writers realized early that the American fabric is not subject to European tailoring, that America has no culture in European terms. But as James said, "The American knows that a good deal remains; what is it that remains—that is his secret, his joke, as one may say. . . ."

The "secret" is evident in the invalidism of their public poses, their exile *in order* to communicate. One learns about America, not from being in Europe as much as from *not* being in America. But this exile, this rebellious detachment, has ambiguous consequences. On the one hand, it affects a dialetical viewpoint, which is to say, it sees the world in terms of primary conflicts. On the other hand, the very symmetry, the *given* drama of such polar conflicts, may be so compelling as to preclude any further analysis or development. A comparison of these two exiles, their experience with the dialectic, not only reflects the cultural history of a half-century, but implies a good deal about the future of the novel.

Baldwin's first paradox is that he uses the Negro, uses him ruthlessly, to show the White Man what the White Man is. Repeatedly in his work, he returns to that image of a Negro hung from a fine Southern tree with his sex cut out. We confront the Negro, we cannot miss him. But we know little about him except that he suffered. We know more, implicitly, about the White Man who left him there. The insights and blind spots of such a technique are illustrated in Baldwin's most ambitious work, *Another Country*.

This novel is populated by a series of characters, or rather couples, as geometrically entangled as Far Eastern erotic sculpture, the only undocumented relationship being that unlovely norm—monogamous, heterosexual marriage. Consider the cast of characters:

Rufus: black jazz drummer, attempts to surmount his ghetto existence by a love affair with a Southern poor white, *Leona*. The attempt to confront, transcend, their past results in her madness and his suicide. This couple is removed from the action relatively early. Subsequent relationships embellish this dazzling affair from other sexual and moral perspectives, through the use of *ficelles*—James's word for characters who, while not self-sustaining, provide *relief* or depth by their juxtaposition to the primary figures of the work.

Vivaldo: white Irish-Italian, unpublished writer, has an affair with *Rufus's* sister, panther-lady, jazz singer, *Ida*. Tempered, perhaps, by the knowledge that their respective talents may gain them escape from the ghetto, *Ida* and *Vivaldo* seem one generation removed from the heat of *Rufus* and *Leona*. They are reincarnations; history is personalized for them through the primary disastrous affair. To some extent, Vivaldo overcomes Leona's naïveté; Ida, her brother's cynicism. "You got to pay your dues," is Ida's theme—and although nothing is resolved, we suspect that in willing to be haunted, they may yet finally afford it.

Then there is *Cass*, blonde upper-class Anglo-Saxon; and her husband, *Richard*, blonde lower-class Polack, high school teacher of Vivaldo, writer. What Cass comes to resent in her husband is not clear—he is disciplined rather than talented perhaps—he does not indulge in the other's frenetic search for a large identity—he actually finishes a book and gets it published. In any case, *Cass* has an affair with *Eric*, ex-Alabama actor, formerly a lover of Rufus and later involved with Vivaldo, then in an interlude awaiting the arrival of his present lover, *Yves*, French, ex-male prostitute. This affair is necessarily brief. *Cass* gets guilty and tells *Richard;* the question of revenge is made properly irrelevant by the knowledge that he has been cuckolded by a queer. We leave him searching out *Vivaldo*, ready to take up, apparently, the aimless rebellion the rest of them find so compelling, the source of his stability defiled. Meanwhile, *Cass* and *Eric* arrange their *Te Deum* in the Museum of Modern Art. The scene is crucial and among the best in the book.

> "Dear Cass . . . how are you?"
> "Dead . . ."
> "You picked a strange place for us to meet . . ."
> "Did I? I just couldn't think of any other place."

And with this they move through the unending anterooms of the modern world—all glass and steel, no texture there—rooms emblazoned with incomprehensible abstractions, cold walls ogled by triumphant myopics, ". . . like tourists in a foreign graveyard." Before an enormous red canvas, stand a boy and girl holding hands, American Gothic against the Apocalypse.

Here, in one scene, is all that distance between Christopher Newman, James's *American,* and more contemporary stuff. For despite Newman's inability to accept his own culture or to fathom a foreign atmosphere no less stifling, he could find solace in the red doors of Notre Dame, as James did in the *Galerie d'Appallon.* By simply standing in the Bellegarde's great hall, Newman could construe the nature of his rebuff; that it was his part to pay his absentee rent and return home.

That is the nostalgic quality of James's characters—they divine their atmosphere, their responses are equal to the situation. They make their peace with a precise if unhappy destiny. But the atmosphere is more opaque for Baldwin's characters, it elicits no response, they simply suffer from it. The museum is no longer teaching machine or urban oasis, any more than bank or hospital, church or train station—their sensitivity, their culture, their very cosmopolitanism is turned against them.

Through this Cass moves, "small, pale, and old fashioned in her hood . . . disenchanted." Eric "wished that he could rescue her, that it was in his power to make her life less hard. But it was only

love which could accomplish the miracle of making a life bearable—
only love, and love itself hopelessly failed; and he had never loved
her. He had used her to find something out about himself. *And
even this was not true.* He had used her in the hope of avoiding a
confrontation with himself."

Cass is pithy as any Jamesian interlocutor. "He can suffer, after
all," she says of Richard. "I told him because . . . that if we were
going to—continue together—we could begin on a new basis with
everything clear between us. But I was wrong—some things cannot be clear . . . or perhaps some things *are* clear, only one won't
face those things."

In that parallelism hangs the book. Tolstoy would have used
those last sentences as his first. The story would have unfolded
from their dichotomy. It is characteristic of modern art that the
thesis is not hung until we have been dragged kicking through
every conceivable blind alley—the self being the sum of the destruction of all false selves.

Echoes of these three relationships reverberate through another
series of *ficelles*. Eric and Yves *en famille* in France, Eric and Vivaldo together for a night, Vivaldo's affair with *Jane*, a no-account
painter, and Ida's with *Ellis*, a white promoter. Ellis and Jane are
coupled as the whores, respectively, of the Commercial and Bohemian worlds. "To have one's pleasure without paying for it,"
Baldwin says elsewhere, "is precisely the way to find oneself reduced to a search for pleasure which grows steadily more desperate
and more grotesque." Baldwin once accused Richard Wright of
substituting violence for sex. He has come full circle.

In the end, things are magnificently unresolved, save for Rufus's
death and Leona's madness. Vivaldo and Ida keep at their work,
their respective therapies, having very little time left to make it before the defensiveness of Greenwich Village will crush them, too.
Cass and Richard have "awoken," only to find themselves "dead."
Undoubtedly, their children will keep them together formally, and
Richard will half-heartedly take up the rebellion where Cass half-
heartedly left it off. Jane finds security with an ad-man, and Ellis,
excitement across the tracks in Harlem. Yves is coming and Eric's
waiting. All end committed to nothing save the endurance of each
other's better knowledge.

If this sounds flip, it is meant to be, for what makes modern tragedy most appalling is not its causality, but its very casualness. Here are the Jews boarding the box cars without resistance.

The irresolution of these destinies, however, has brought some critics down hard on Baldwin. The charge is formlessness. But if *Another Country* is formless, it has that in common with this nation's greatest literature. In the final scene, Eric goes to meet Yves at Idlewild.

> Yves . . . passed his examination with no trouble, and in a very short time; his passport was eventually stamped and handed back to him, with a grin and a small joke, the meaning but not the good nature of which escaped him. Then he was in a vaster hall, waiting for his luggage, with Eric above him, smiling down on him through glass. Then even his luggage belonged to him again, and he strode through the barriers, more high-hearted than he had even been as a child, into that city which the people from heaven had made their home.

That is not the language of Henry James, the understated snippet of dialogue or restrained image which brings things to a close. It is the language of Gatsby and the Green Light, Huck Finn, "striking out for the territory," Ishmael, picked up, alone, to tell the tale— the picaresque open-end of American Literature. (As Robert A. Bone points out in a brilliant study [which is concluded in this volume], Baldwin, "in moments of high emotion," consistently reverts to his formal, more elaborate church-oriented narrative, rather than to any dialect or colloquial idiom.)

For a moment we are placated; he has gotten out of it in a traditional manner. But then we realize that in this ecstatic scene, no one is fleeing injustice with high hopes, Yves is no Lafayette on the beach; this is no rendezvous with destiny, but a discomforting liaison. The visionary rhetoric is utterly undercut.

So the legend of America as refuge for the oppressed, opportunity for the pure in heart, is invoked only to be exposed. From the very first, he is saying, our vision has been parochial. We have not accounted for the variety of man's motives, the underside of our settlers, the cost of a new life. The plague has come over as part of the baggage, and we will be sick until we isolate that cargo and deal with it. The back dues compound every day. If *Another Country* is formless, it is so because it rejects the theories of history available to it.

There is something further, however, an inadequacy which is worth pointing out, as it relates not only to Baldwin, but to modern literature itself.

What about the progenitors of such knowledge? The characters that set *Another Country* in motion, Leona and Rufus? It is what Baldwin does not know, or say, about them which is interesting, for they must bear the primary burden, they are the myth which the other couples mime. As myths, Baldwin tends to monumentalize them, give them stature by arresting their development. Like Greek royalty, their personality is gradually subsumed by the enormity of the crime which killed them.

But who are they? Rufus Scott has that ethereal sensitivity of the modern hero, half-adolescent, half-prophet, that *powerless, feeling young man* celebrated, apparently, because he rejects a success already denied him—the man who in Norman Mailer's words would "affect history by the sheer force of his sentiments." Or so the logic goes. But really, he is a monument from the very first, he is that Negro hanging from the tree with his sex cut out.

The fact is, that Rufus is nothing but his own potential, and the world is simply what thwarts it. He is a brilliantly rendered testament. But he is not a character. What *he* can't do and why *they* won't let him, is more vague than mysterious. He is, if you will, the Seymour Glass of his class, his virtue postulated by his lesser apostles. It is significant that although Rufus is a musician, we never hear him play. As with Seymour's alleged poetry, we await the aria that never comes.

And Leona? Poor white trash Isolde? Significantly, the only character in the book not devoted in some way to the arts. Symbols, representation, mean nothing to her. It is commerce, communication in the most direct sense, that she lives. "Do you love me?" everyman's saxophone asks. Leona says, "Don't hurt me." The pale white liberal; impotent (I ain't gonna have no more babies), platitudinous (it don't matter what two people's color is so long as they love each other), ineradicably guilty. She tries to love Rufus because she needs him, and he won't let her because it smacks of retribution. Her effort, pathetic, styleless, is for nothing. She is committed to an institution. But that is only the legal acknowledgment. If Baldwin does not see what Rufus might become, he does not see what Leona *is*. She does not go crazy; she has been mad from the beginning. As characters, they *go* nowhere; they die of nothing more than their own abstraction.

"What they (Negroes) hold in common is their precarious, their unutterably painful relation to the white world," Baldwin says. What the characters of *Another Country* hold in common is their precarious relation to a world which is defined by little more than its victims' resentment. One by one, we come upon them, hung from their respective trees, but the executioner never appears; like *Godot*, his name is simply invoked to "explain things." What is explicitly absent in Baldwin's politics—the differentiation between enemies, the priorities and strategies of rebellion—is implicitly absent in his literature.

To structure the dialogue in this way has its dramatic usefulness. The conflicts are elucidated in all their hopeless solipsism. But the consequence is also to make development, in terms of plot, psychology, or character, impossible. He is overwhelmed by the eloquence of his own dialectic. He has reached that moment which defines much of modern fiction—when the characters start to repeat themselves endlessly. Recapitulation of this sort has its irony—upon which the theatre of the absurd has capitalized—but artistically, it is also a dead end.

To understand how an artist can get into this situation, *Another Country* must be considered the result of a long and certainly uplifting process. Baldwin's progress as an artist has been his ability to articulate, confront, his central problems as a man and a writer. He tells us of his exile to Europe, with little but recordings of Bessie Smith and his shame. There, gradually, he came to grips with the central conflicts of his background, his love-hate affairs with religion, sex, color, America. In *Go Tell It on the Mountain*, the futile beauty of the Negro church is dealt with by incorporating its esthetic while rejecting it as an institution. He learns to use the jagged Negro folk poetry and religious rhetoric, to counter the urbane elegance of his Jamesian style. In *Giovanni's Room*, "the male prison" is dealt with as the "church-as-jail" by using the ambiguities of sexual desire as the proof-text for a larger rebellion. In *Notes of a Native Son*, in *Nobody Knows My Name*, Baldwin discovers himself further. What began as a crippling disgust with both his race and country, as an *American*, a *Negro*, becomes a subtle distinctive pride in each as *americanegro*. In these essays, he finds a unique and telling voice—neither before nor since are his categories so precisely focused, nor his language so controlled. He has "his secret, his joke." He returns.

Such progress is apparent in *Another Country*, but it is a work of a different order. It is less explicitly therapeutic, more ambitious. It is the very repetition, the surface perversity of the encounters, that gradually makes perversity irrelevant. For this is not at all a book about interracial affairs, homosexual affairs, adulterous affairs, but about *affairs*—it evolves in the same way that *Portrait of a Lady*, say, unfolds upon the loom of marriage. The various approaches, styles, perspectives are secondary. They all need the same thing if they face different obstacles, they all pay the same dues. Everyone hits bottom in his own way and that is that. Yves and Eric's liaison is significant on one level of irony, but ultimately it is of no peculiar issue. Their final significance is that they simply carry on the central burden of the book, the frantic attempt to know something of one another. Perversion is no single act; but rather, *any* unaffecting love.

Baldwin has constructed his terrible dialectic; he has drawn up the battle lines so that we may never be safe again. But what he has done, in scrupulously avoiding everybody's social protest novel, is to write everybody's existential novel. The problem is more than being fashionable. For one thing, as Ralph Ellison has shown us, the Negro as a character has all the clichés of the existential malady built-in. The absurdity of his status, the necessity of his rebellion, is culturally given. He is defined as much by others' misconceptions of him as by any self-perception, he is still what he always has been in our literature—that most immediate example of God's default. Contemporary literature in this respect is unique only in that it believes God was wrong.

This kind of status also has its uses. James's characters have an extraordinary freedom based on money—and it is no accident that Baldwin's characters are similarly unaffected by conventional economic problems. This is not because they are more spiritual, but simply because this is as accurate an index of modern affluent society as James's analysis of the international aristocracy. In short, the economics of both situations are only manifestations of more significant and complex problems. Rufus did not kill himself because he did not have enough to eat when he was a child, but because he understood the dimensions of ignorance and fear, one consequence of which was to affect his diet. Unhampered by the obvious, Baldwin has cut through the pop-sociology of his time to the roots of contemporary frustration—the curse not of slavery, but leisure; not of organization, but alienation; not of social evil, but of individual love. Baldwin's assertion that we are all second-class citizens in our existential dilemma, that the terms of our exclusion are similar, is his greatest achievement. In the end, his protagonists are not black anymore than we are white.

But such status may also be abused. For after self-consciousness, after all the billboards are down, then what? The message of this existentialism is the equality of guilt, the equality of men before no law—but when the rebellion has been justified, then what happens? Experience under these assumptions is predictable, sensibility has but one consequence. To say that the self is not what we commonly thought, even to say it again and again, is not to say what the self is.

"We have so completely debunked the old idea of the Self," Saul Bellow has said, "that we can hardly continue in the same way." And Baldwin cannot continue in the same way, if he is to further confront the problems he has set himself in *Another Country*.

Another Country is our country, real, repressed, and envisioned, and Baldwin's return to it does not break down the parallel with James in the least. His point of view remains that of the exile. Under existential assumptions, self-exile, to paraphrase a politician, is not a choice, but a condition. It is the condition of that *powerless, feeling young man,* an echo of that "reaction against a mistake," that dangling emasculate Negro, that rage to be "other almost anyhow."

But how do you differentiate when everybody is "other" anyway? Why do Rufus and Richard give up? Why do Ida and Vivaldo persevere? These are ambiguities in the work that cannot be justified by saying that life is ambiguous as well. The underground man is pretty thin fare by this time. Too many of us live there now to be celebrated as either indicative or unique. "There is no structure," Baldwin says, "that he [the artist] can build to keep out self-knowledge." But he has not yet demonstrated, except in his essays, that the artist can build a structure to *use* self-knowledge.

In this regard, he may profit once again from his mentor. For *Another Country* is as much a *vie en provence* as, say, *The Bos-*

tonians. And both mark similar stages of maturity for their authors. Both books tend to abstract national character through a microcosm; an abstraction which can only be justified by elaboration in later work. It is a question of giving corroborative detail to a general observation, rather than letting the generalization, powerful as it may be, stand for the detail. For example, when James says of Miss Birdseye that "the whole moral history of Boston was reflected in her displaced spectacles," he is indulging himself in a sort of phrase which saves the book from the commonplace, but commits the author eventually to a more subtle analysis. With this in mind, consider this paragraph from *Another Country:*

> . . . Rufus walked, one of the fallen—for the weight of the city was murderous—one of those who had been crushed on the day, which was every day, these towers fall. Entirely alone and dying of it, he was part of an unprecedented multitude . . . that could scarcely bear their knowledge. . . .

Moral histories ought to be exemplified, not simply invoked. It is the individual who defines the multitude, not the other way around.

Although James's personal conflicts do not seem as compelling (modern) as Baldwin's, he was certainly faulted for the same sort of abstraction. Eliot maintained that he failed to "detect his own characters." Gide spoke of his personages as "winged busts." Edmund Wilson at one time was moved to proclaim that Hyacinth Robinson of the *Princess Casamassima* died of "the class struggle," but F. W. Dupee is more to the point in stating that he died of a "poverty of ideas." What he means is that Hyacinth is without the insight to sustain himself as a character. His impotence is as unexamined as Rufus's appetite. They are too good for the world and too abstract for literature.

Yet James refused to be satisfied by the type of the *powerless, feeling young man,* for he knew how easy it was for him to uphold such a one, and how graciously his audience would accept him. He was too involved in his own cultural adventure to settle for the drama of limited character and obvious dichotomy. His concern can be seen in his notebooks—"the web of consciousness," his own metaphor, replaces the dialectic as a structural principle. Whatever the argument over the convolutions of the later style, the consequences of his continued exile, it is apparent that the later heroes of sensibility are transfigured, and again I use his own words, into "personalities of transcendent value." He is not satisfied simply to doom his characters in his later work, not because they ought not to go down, but because that story was written—those conflicts were charted—and now the problem was to develop the internal relations between the sides he had so artfully chosen. It was a question of creating characters sufficiently complex to sustain them beyond the dialectical conflict which created them.

The turning point in James's career was perhaps *The Ambassadors,* in which Strether renounces his cautiousness in the famous exhortation, "Get all the experience you can." This does not refer to a more romantic life-style; it is more like the Turgenev character in *Virgin Soil* who says "I could not simplify myself." As usual, James reinforces this character's particular dialogue with an unspoken generalization, "it was the proportions that were changed, and the proportions were at all times, he philosophized, the very conditions of perception, the terms of thought." The remarkable thing about these later characters is that they refuse to draw conclusions that would preclude further investigation on their part, and for that matter, further involvement for the reader. The galling thing about Baldwin's characters—and most "existential" heroes—is that they are so susceptible to conclusions which define them immediately. It is not that their truth is bitter, it is that their truth comes so easily—however hard it may be to shake it. In fact, they are all *ficelles.*

The quality of the later James lies in the tension between characters. Who is guilty? Who is innocent? Our final knowledge is that Paris, France, and Wollett, Mass., are not knowable without the other, that the categories with which we began the book no longer can apply. Radical innocence and guileless evil are neither opposed nor reconciled—they are intermeshed in a genuine mystery. Baldwin is shocking; not yet terrifying. What he has shown us is that everyone is guilty. This is the true paradox of the existential hero, for in all his hefty insistence that rebellion is justified, he seems to end up lacking the energy to achieve the *engagement* to which he pays his coffee-house lip-service.

Henry James was able to achieve what his notebooks anticipated: the reclamation of large areas of social experience, the transformamation of these abstractions into material for the imagination. Baldwin has yet to progress beyond the initial encounter. He has, most powerfully, given us an opportunity to test our preconceptions, but that ultimately is social science, not literature.

The question remains, why pick on Baldwin when these are questions to be applied to modern fiction generally? Why does he take the burden of the breakthrough?

For one thing, Baldwin has progressed in each of his works, his dialectic has become progressively more refined. He has shown a flexibility and perseverance equal to our most influential artists. Further, and almost alone, he has continued to confront the unmanageable questions of modern society, rather than creating a nuclear family in which semantic fantasies may be enacted with no reference to the larger world except that it stinks. There can be no escape into technique or historiography. It will not do for him to remember something else. He must continue to find out about himself. It is his actual experience, perhaps, even more than the shaping of it, which will be crucial. To bring us to the door in Rufus's name will not be enough next time.

Baldwin's experience is unique among our artists in that his artistic achievements mesh so precisely with his historical circumstances. He is that nostalgic type—an artist speaking for a genuinely visible revolution. He is first in line for that Nirvana of American liberals, a Ministry of Culture. As with James, his problem is to give artistic life to the critical insights of his prefaces, his notebooks, in short, to develop characters which have a subtle and various consciousness equal to the omniscient, cranky narrator of the essays. This particular problem accounts for the failure of both artists as playwrights. Theatrical success depends upon rendering the particulars of a character through bald dialogue. Only rarely can a narrator amplify a character through abstract description; no disembodied voice can bridge the gap between an idea and its personification as in an essay or narrative literature. For those obsessed with the dialectic, for those whose characters are forever battling their own abstraction, the proscenium marks a treacherous zone.

Yet the very critical faculties which confine a sensibility may liberate it in the long run. Baldwin knows more than he has yet translated into literature. Like his mentor, he has used the essay, not as exposition in lieu of a work of larger intent, but as a testing ground for his fiction. Consider these notes of a native son:

> I could not be certain whether I was really rich or really poor, really black or really white, really male or really female, really talented or a fraud, really strong or merely stubborn. In short, I had become an American. . . .

. . . at that time it seemed only too clear that love had gone out of the world, and not, as I had thought once, because I was poor and ugly and obscure, but precisely because I was no longer any of these things.

These remarkable observations are a fit foundation for Baldwin's future development.

Critics are at their most useless when they try to second-guess the proper conditions of an artist's experience, but is it too much to suggest that an American artist can finally make use of his notoriety? Is it not possible that the invasions of his privacy, the mass meetings, the TV appearance, the form letters, the suspicion of his protégés, the galling affection of his enemies, cannot provide a further insight into our society? Baldwin has had his winter of a hundred dinner parties. "Try to be one of those," James says, "upon whom nothing is lost." What happens when a poet becomes an acknowledged legislator? What happens to the rebel who finds that the price of one's resistance is that one has no reality beyond the resistance? That has always been the paradox of our rebels, and it has never been explored. And does not this paradox speak to our condition more than any ritualistic homage to the absurd? Is not the real "existential" dilemma that of this sensitive man who is never alone, engaged even against his will, whose paradox lies in his very power?

"The moral is that the flower of art blooms only where the soil is deep, that . . ." it takes a great deal of literature to produce a little history, that it needs a complex writer to set a social machinery in motion.

Notes on a Native Son

by Eldridge Cleaver

After reading a couple of James Baldwin's books, I began experiencing that continuous delight one feels upon discovering a fascinating, brilliant talent on the scene, a talent capable of penetrating so profoundly into one's own little world that one knows oneself to have been unalterably changed and *liberated*, liberated from the frustrating grasp of whatever devils happen to possess one. Being a Negro, I have found this to be a rare and infrequent experience, for few of my black brothers and sisters here in America have achieved the power, which James Baldwin calls his revenge, which outlasts kingdoms: the power of doing whatever cats like Baldwin do when combining the alphabet with the volatile elements of his soul. (And, like it or not, a black man, unless he has become irretrievably "white-minded," responds with an additional dimension of his being to the articulated experience of another black—in spite of the universality of human experience.)

I, as I imagine many others did and still do, lusted for anything that Baldwin had written. It would have been a gas for me to sit on a pillow beneath the womb of Baldwin's typewriter and catch each newborn page as it entered this world of ours. I was delighted that Baldwin, with those great big eyes of his, which one thought to be fixedly focused on the macrocosm, could also pierce the microcosm. And although he was so full of sound, he was not a noisy writer like Ralph Ellison. He placed so much of my own experience, which I thought I had understood, into new perspective.

Gradually, however, I began to feel uncomfortable about something in Baldwin. I was disturbed upon becoming aware of an aversion in my heart to part of the song he sang. Why this was so,

I was unable at first to say. Then I read *Another Country*, and I knew why my love for Baldwin's vision had become ambivalent.

Long before, I had become a student of Norman Mailer's *The White Negro*, which seemed to me to be prophetic and penetrating in its understanding of the psychology involved in the accelerating confrontation of black and white in America. I was therefore personally insulted by Baldwin's flippant, schoolmarmish dismissal of *The White Negro*. Baldwin committed a literary crime by his arrogant repudiation of one of the few gravely important expressions of our time. *The White Negro* may contain an excess of esoteric verbal husk, but one can forgive Mailer for that because of the solid kernel of truth he gave us. After all, it is the baby we want and not the blood of afterbirth. Mailer described, in that incisive essay, the first important chinks in the "mountain of white supremacy"—important because it shows the depth of ferment, on a personal level, in the white world. People are feverishly, and at great psychic and social expense, seeking *fundamental and irrevocable liberation*—and, what is more important, *are succeeding in escaping*—from the big white lies that compose the monolithic myth of White Supremacy/Black Inferiority, in a desperate attempt on the part of a new generation of white Americans to enter into the cosmopolitan egalitarian spirit of the twentieth century. But let us examine the reasoning that lies behind Baldwin's attack on Mailer.

There is in James Baldwin's work the most grueling, agonizing, total hatred of the blacks, particularly of himself, and the most shameful, fanatical, fawning, sycophantic love of the whites that one can find in the writings of any black American writer of note in our time. This is an appalling contradiction and the implications of it are vast.

A rereading of *Nobody Knows My Name* cannot help but convince the most avid of Baldwin's admirers of the hatred for blacks permeating his writings. In the essay "Princes and Powers," Baldwin's antipathy toward the black race is shockingly clear. The essay is Baldwin's interpretation of the Conference of Black Writers and Artists which met in Paris in September 1956. The portrait of Baldwin that comes through his words is that of a mind in unrelenting opposition to the efforts of solemn, dedicated black men who have undertaken the enormous task of rejuvenating and reclaiming the shattered psyches and culture of the black people, a people scattered over the continents of the world and the islands of the seas, where they exist in the mud of the floor of the foul dungeon into which the world has been transformed by the whites.

In his report of the conference, Baldwin, the reluctant black, dragging his feet at every step, could only ridicule the vision and efforts of these great men and heap scorn upon them, reserving his compliments—all of them lefthanded—for the speakers at the conference who were themselves rejected and booed by the other conferees because of their reactionary, sycophantic views. Baldwin felt called upon to pop his cap pistol in a duel with Aimé Césaire, the big gun from Martinique. Indirectly, Baldwin was defending his first love—the white man. But the revulsion which Baldwin felt for the blacks at this conference, who were glorying in their blackness, seeking and showing their pride in Negritude and the African Personality, drives him to self-revealing sortie after sortie, so obvious in "Princes and Powers." Each successive sortie, however, becomes more expensive than the last one, because to score each time he has to go a little farther out on the limb, and it takes him a little longer each time to hustle back to the cover and camouflage of the perfumed smoke screen of his prose. Now and then we catch a glimpse of his little jive ass—his big eyes peering back over his shoulder in the mischievous retreat of a child sneak-thief from a cookie jar.

In the autobiographical notes of *Notes of a Native Son*, Baldwin is frank to confess that, in growing into his version of manhood in Harlem, he discovered that, since his African heritage had been wiped out and was not accessible to him, he would appropriate the white man's heritage and make it his own. This terrible reality, central to the psychic stance of all American Negroes, revealed to Baldwin that he hated and feared white people. Then he says: "This did not mean that I loved black people; on the contrary, I despised them, possibly because they failed to produce Rembrandt." The psychic distance between love and hate could be the mechanical difference between a smile and a sneer, or it could be the journey of a nervous impulse from the depths of one's brain to the tip of one's toe. But this impulse in its path through North American nerves may, if it is honest, find the passage disputed: may find the leap from the fiber of hate to that of love too taxing on its meager store of energy—and so the long trip back may never be completed, may end in a reconnaissance, a compromise, and then a lie.

Self-hatred takes many forms; sometimes it can be detected by no one, not by the keenest observer, not by the self-hater himself, not by his most intimate friends. Ethnic self-hate is even more difficult to detect. But in American Negroes, this ethnic self-hatred often takes the bizarre form of a racial death-wish, with many and elusive manifestations. Ironically, it provides much of the impetus behind the motivations of integration. And the attempt to suppress or deny such drives in one's psyche leads many American Negroes to become ostentatious separationists, Black Muslims, and back-to-Africa advocates. It is no wonder that Elijah Muhammad could conceive of the process of controlling evolution whereby the white race was brought into being. According to Elijah, about 6300 years ago all the people of the earth were Original Blacks. Secluded on the island of Patmos, a mad black scientist by the name of Yacub set up the machinery for grafting whites out of blacks through the operation of a birth-control system. The population on the island of Patmos was 59,999 and whenever a couple on this island wanted to get married they were only allowed to do so if there was a difference in their color, so that by mating black with those in the population of a brownish color and brown with brown—but never black with black—all traces of the black were eventually eliminated; the process was repeated until all brown was eliminated, leaving only men of the red race; the red was bleached out, leaving only yellow; then the yellow was bleached out, and only white was left. Thus Yacub, who was long since dead, because this whole process took hundreds of years, had finally succeeded in creating the white devil with the blue eyes of death.

This myth of the creation of the white race, called "Yacub's History," is an inversion of the racial death-wish of American Negroes. Yacub's plan is still being followed by many Negroes today. Quite simply, many Negroes believe, as the principle of assimilation into white America implies, that the race problem in America cannot be settled until all traces of the black race are eliminated. Toward this end, many Negroes loathe the very idea of two very dark Negroes mating. The children, they say, will come out ugly. What they mean is that the children are sure to be black, and this is not desirable. From the widespread use of cosmetics to bleach the black out of one's skin and other concoctions to take Africa out of one's hair, to the extreme, resorted to by more Negroes than one might wish to believe, of undergoing nose-thinning and lip-clipping operations, the racial death-wish of American Negroes—Yacub's goal—takes its terrible toll. What has been happening for the past four hundred years is that the white man, through his access to black women, has been pumping his blood and genes into the blacks, has been diluting the blood and genes of the blacks —i.e., has been fulfilling Yacub's plan and accelerating the Negroes' racial death-wish.

The case of James Baldwin aside for a moment, it seems that many Negro homosexuals, acquiescing in this racial death-wish, are outraged and frustrated because in their sickness they are unable to have a baby by a white man. The cross they have to bear is that, already bending over and touching their toes for the white man, the fruit of their miscegenation is not the little half-white offspring of their dreams but an increase in the unwinding of their nerves— though they redouble their efforts and intake of the white man's sperm.

In this land of dichotomies and disunited opposites, those truly concerned with the resurrection of black Americans have had eternally to deal with black intellectuals who have become their own opposites, taking on all of the behavior patterns of their enemy, vices and virtues, in an effort to aspire to alien standards in all respects. The gulf between an audacious, bootlicking Uncle Tom and an intellectual buckdancer is filled only with sophistication and style. On second thought, Uncle Tom comes off much cleaner here because usually he is just trying to survive, choosing to pretend to be something other than his true self in order to please the white man and thus receive favors. Whereas the intellectual sycophant does not pretend to be other than he actually is, but hates what he is and seeks to redefine himself in the image of his white idols. He becomes a white man in a black body. A self-willed, automated slave, he becomes the white man's most valuable tool in oppressing other blacks.

The black homosexual, when his twist has a racial nexus, is an extreme embodiment of this contradiction. The white man has deprived him of his masculinity, castrated him in the center of his burning skull, and when he submits to this change and takes the white man for his lover as well as Big Daddy, he focuses on "whiteness" all the love in his pent up soul and turns the razor edge of hatred against "blackness"—upon himself, what he is, and all those who look like him, remind him of himself. He may even hate the darkness of night.

The racial death-wish is manifested as the driving force in James Baldwin. His hatred for blacks, even as he pleads what he conceives as their cause, makes him the apotheosis of the dilemma in the ethos of the black bourgeoisie who have completely rejected their African heritage, consider the loss irrevocable, and refuse to look again in that direction. This is the root of Baldwin's violent repudiation of Mailer's *The White Negro.*

To understand what is at stake here, and to understand it in terms of the life of this nation, is to know the central fact that the relationship between black and white in America is a power equation, a power struggle, and that this power struggle is not only manifested in the aggregate (civil rights, black nationalism, etc.) but also in the interpersonal relationships, actions, and reactions between blacks and whites where taken into account. When those "two lean cats," Baldwin and Mailer, met in a French living room, it was precisely this power equation that was at work.

It is fascinating to read (in *Nobody Knows My Name*) in what terms this power equation was manifested in Baldwin's immediate reaction to that meeting: "And here we were, suddenly, circling around each other. We liked each other at once, but each was frightened that the other would pull rank. He could have pulled rank on me because he was more famous and *had more money* and also *because he was white;* but I could have pulled rank on him precisely because I was black and knew more about that periphery he so helplessly maligns in *The White Negro* than he could ever hope to know." [Italics added.]

Pulling rank, it would seem, is a very dangerous business, especially when the troops have mutinied and the basis of one's authority, or rank, is devoid of that interdictive power and has become suspect. One would think that for Baldwin, of all people, these hues of black and white were no longer armed with the power to intimidate—and if one thought this, one would be exceedingly wrong: for behind the structure of the thought of Baldwin's quoted above, there lurks the imp of Baldwin's unwinding, of his tension between love and hate—love of the white and hate of the black. And when we dig into this tension we will find that when those "two lean cats" crossed tracks in that French living room, one was a Pussy Cat, the other a Tiger. Baldwin's purr was transmitted magnificently in *The Fire Next Time.* But his work is the fruit of a tree with a poison root. Such succulent fruit, such a painful tree, what a malignant root!

It is ironic, but fascinating for what it reveals about the ferment in the North American soul in our time, that Norman Mailer, the white boy, and James Baldwin, the black boy, encountered each other in the eye of a social storm, traveling in opposite directions; the white boy, with knowledge of white Negroes, was traveling toward a confrontation with the black, with Africa; while the black boy, with a white mind, was on his way to Europe. Baldwin's nose, like the North-seeking needle on a compass, is forever pointed toward his adopted fatherland, Europe, his by intellectual osmosis and in Africa's stead. What he says of Aimé Césaire, one of the greatest black writers of the twentieth century, and intending it as an ironic rebuke, that "he had penetrated into the heart of the great wilderness which was Europe and stolen the sacred fire . . . which . . . was . . . the assurance of his power," seems only too clearly to speak more about Peter than it does about Paul. What Baldwin seems to forget is that Césaire explains that fire, whether sacred or profane, burns. In Baldwin's case, though the fire could not burn the black off his face, it certainly did burn it out of his heart.

I am not interested in denying anything to Baldwin. I, like the entire nation, owe a great debt to him. But throughout the range of his work, from *Go Tell It on the Mountain,* through *Notes of a Native Son, Nobody Knows My Name, Another Country,* to *The Fire Next Time,* all of which I treasure, there is a decisive quirk in Baldwin's vision which corresponds to his relationship to black people and to masculinity. It was this same quirk, in my opinion, that compelled Baldwin to slander Rufus Scott in *Another Country,* venerate André Gide, repudiate *The White Negro,* and drive the blade of Brutus into the corpse of Richard Wright. As Baldwin has said in *Nobody Knows My Name,* "I think that I know something about the American masculinity which most men of my generation do not know because they have not been menaced by it in the way I have been." O.K., Sugar, but isn't it true that Rufus Scott, the weak, craven-hearted ghost of *Another Country,* bears the same relation to Bigger Thomas of *Native Son,* the black rebel of the ghetto and a man, as you yourself bore to the fallen giant, Richard Wright, a rebel and a man?

Somewhere in one of his books, Richard Wright describes an

encounter between a ghost and several young Negroes. The young Negroes rejected the homosexual, and this was Wright alluding to a classic, if cruel, example of a ubiquitous phenomenon in the black ghettos of America: the practice by Negro youths of going "punk-hunting." This practice of seeking out homosexuals on the prowl, rolling them, beating them up, seemingly just to satisfy some savage impulse to inflict pain on the specific target selected, the "social outcast," seems to me to be not unrelated, in terms of the psychological mechanisms involved, to the ritualistic lynchings and castrations inflicted on Southern blacks by Southern whites. This was, as I recall, one of Wright's few comments on the subject of homosexuality.

I think it can safely be said that the men in Wright's books, albeit shackled with a form of impotence, were strongly heterosexual. Their heterosexuality was implied rather than laboriously stated or emphasized; it was taken for granted, as we all take men until something occurs to make us know otherwise. And Bigger Thomas, Wright's greatest creation, was a man in violent, though inept, rebellion against the stifling, murderous, totalitarian white world. There was no trace in Bigger of a Martin Luther King-type self-effacing love for his oppressors. For example, Bigger would have been completely baffled, as most Negroes are today, at Baldwin's advice to his nephew (*The Fire Next Time*), concerning white people: "You must accept them *and accept them with love.* For these innocent people have no other hope." [Italics added.]

Rufus Scott, a pathetic wretch who indulged in the white man's pastime of committing suicide, who let a white bisexual homosexual fuck him in his ass, and who took a Southern Jezebel for his woman, with all that these tortured relationships imply, was the epitome of a black eunuch who has completely submitted to the white man. Yes, Rufus was a psychological freedom rider, turning the ultimate cheek, murmuring like a ghost, *"You took the best so why not take the rest,"* which has absolutely nothing to do with the way Negroes have managed to survive here in the hells of North America! This all becomes very clear from what we learn of Erich, the arch-ghost of *Another Country,* of the depths of his alienation from his body and the source of his need: "And it had taken him almost until this very moment, on the eve of his departure, to begin to recognize that part of Rufus' great power over him had to do with the past which Erich had buried in some deep, dark place; was connected

with himself, in Alabama, *when I wasn't nothing but a child;* with
the cold white people and the warm black people, warm at least for
him. . . ."

So, too, who cannot wonder at the source of such audacious madness as moved Baldwin to make this startling remark about Richard
Wright, in his ignoble essay "Alas, Poor Richard": "In my own
relations with him, I was always exasperated by his notions of society, politics, and history, for they seemed to me utterly fanciful.
I never believed that he had any real sense of how a society is put
together."

Richard Wright is dead and Baldwin is alive and with us. Baldwin says that Richard Wright held notions that were utterly fanciful, and Baldwin is an honorable man.

> O judgment; thou are fled to
> brutish beasts,
> And men have lost their reason!

Wright has no need, as Caesar did, of an outraged Antony to plead
his cause: his life and his work are his shield against the mellow
thrust of Brutus' blade. The good that he did, unlike Caesar's, will
not be interred with his bones. It is, on the contrary, only the living
who can be harmed by Brutus.

Baldwin says that in Wright's writings violence sits enthroned
where sex should be. If this is so, then it is only because in the
North American reality hate holds sway in love's true province.
And it is only through a rank perversion that the artist, whose duty
is to tell us the truth, can turn the two-dollar trick of wedding violence to love and sex to hate—if, to achieve this end, one has basely
to transmute rebellion into lamblike submission—*"You took the
best,"* sniveled Rufus, *"so why not take the rest?"* Richard Wright
was not ghost enough to achieve this cruel distortion. With him,
sex, being not a spectator sport or a panacea but the sacred vehicle
of life and love, is itself sacred. And the America which Wright
knew and which *is,* is not the Garden of Eden but its opposite.
Baldwin, embodying in his art the self-flagellating policy of Martin
Luther King, and giving out falsely the news that the Day of the
Ghost has arrived, pulled it off in *Another Country.*

Of all black American novelists, and indeed of all American novelists of any hue, Richard Wright reigns supreme for his profound
political, economic, and social reference. Wright had the ability,

like Dreiser, of harnessing the gigantic, overwhelming environmental forces and focusing them, with pinpoint sharpness, on individuals and their acts as they are caught up in the whirlwind of the savage, anarchistic sweep of life, love, death, and hate, pain, hope, pleasure, and despair across the face of a nation and the world. But, ah! "O masters," it is Baldwin's work which is so void of a political, economic, or even a social reference. His characters all seem to be fucking and sucking in a vacuum. Baldwin has a superb touch when he speaks of human beings, when he is inside of them—especially his homosexuals—but he flounders when he looks beyond the skin; whereas Wright's forte, it seems to me, was in reflecting the intricate mechanisms of a social organization, its functioning as a unit.

Baldwin's essay on Richard Wright reveals that he despised—not Richard Wright, but his masculinity. He cannot confront the stud in others—except that he must either submit to it or destroy it. And he was not about to bow to a *black* man. Wright understood and lived the truth of what Norman Mailer meant when he said ". . . for being a man is the continuing battle of one's life, and one loses a bit of manhood with every stale compromise to the authority of any power in which one does not believe." Baldwin, compromised beyond getting back by the white man's *power*, which is real and which has nothing to do with *authority*, but to which Baldwin has ultimately succumbed psychologically, is totally unable to extricate himself from that horrible pain. It is the scourge of his art, because the only way out for him is psychologically to embrace Africa, the land of his fathers, which he utterly refuses. to do. He has instead resorted to a despicable underground guerrilla war, waged on paper, against black masculinity, playing out the racial death-wish of Yacub, reaching, I think, a point where Mailer hits the spot: "Driven into defiance, it is natural if regrettable, that many homosexuals go to the direction of assuming that there is something intrinsically superior in homosexuality, and carried far enough it is a viewpoint which is as stultifying, as ridiculous, and as anti-human as the heterosexual's prejudice."

I, for one, do not think homosexuality is the latest advance over heterosexuality on the scale of human evolution. Homosexuality is a sickness, just as are baby-rape or wanting to become the head of General Motors.

A grave danger faces this nation, of which we are as yet unaware.

And it is precisely this danger which Baldwin's work conceals; indeed, leads us away from. We are engaged in the deepest, the most fundamental revolution and reconstruction which men have ever been called upon to make in their lives, and which they absolutely cannot escape or avoid except at the peril of the very continued existence of human life on this planet. The time of the sham is over, and the cheek of the suffering saint must no longer be turned twice to the brute. The titillation of the guilt complexes of bored white liberals leads to doom. The grotesque hideousness of what is happening to us is reflected in this remark by Murray Kempton, quoted in *The Realist:* "When I was a boy Stepin Fetchit was the only Negro actor who worked regularly in the movies. . . . The fashion changes, but I sometimes think that Malcolm X and, to a degree even James Baldwin, are *our* Stepin Fetchits."

Yes, the fashion does change. "Will the machinegunners please step forward," said LeRoi Jones in a poem. "The machine gun on the corner," wrote Richard Wright, "is the symbol of the twentieth century." The embryonic spirit of kamikaze, real and alive, grows each day in the black man's heart and there are dreams of Nat Turner's legacy. The ghost of John Brown is creeping through suburbia. And I wonder if James Chaney said, as Andrew Goodman and Michael Schwerner stood helplessly watching, as the grizzly dogs crushed his bones with savage blows of chains—did poor James say, after Rufus Scott—"*You took the best, so why not take the rest?*" Or did he turn to his white brothers, seeing their plight, and say, after Baldwin, "That's your problem, baby!"

I say, after Mailer, "There's a shit-storm coming."

The "Stink" of Reality: Mothers and Whores in James Baldwin's Fiction

by Charlotte Alexander

In the parting scene between the two men in *Giovanni's Room,* Giovanni accuses David of never having loved anyone, including Hella, the American sweetheart for whom he is now attempting to break with Giovanni, his lover.

> You never have loved anyone, I am sure you never will! You love your purity, you love your mirror—you are just like a little virgin, you walk around with your hands in front of you as though you had some precious metal, gold, silver, rubies, maybe *diamonds* down there between your legs! You will never give it to anybody, you will never let anobody *touch* it—man *or* woman. You want to be *clean.* You think you came here covered with soap and you think you will go out covered with soap—and you do not want to *stink,* not even for five minutes, in the meantime.

Although Giovanni's anger stems from the present crisis in which David refuses to continue their homosexual relationship, it highlights David's inability throughout the novel to commit himself to anyone, and focuses on his perpetual flight, flight now and then arrested by the Hellas or the Giovannis. The Italian's words also suggest that David's behavior is sexually, perhaps emotionally, untouchable, virginal: to remain *clean* is to keep a distance, possibly to cling to innocence; to *stink,* on the other hand, is to become involved, touching and being touched, and to risk loss of purity or control. But Baldwin's characters seldom can confront this "stink" of reality in a reassuring way, and Giovanni's speech gives two hints as to what often comes between them and their contentment.

In James Baldwin's fiction, physical intimacy—complicated in this instance from *Giovanni's Room* by the ambivalence of David's sexuality—is the means (potentially) to emotional fulfillment. But the experience of meaningful physical intimacy in a world measured by any standard of reality brings with it risk and mundanity, because one's partner is separate and partly unpredictable, and also because the external universe may be uncontrollable as well as stupidly mundane. Hence Giovanni's accusation that David is selfish and naive, that he wants the one—a "clean" yet satisfying emotional attachment—without the other, the inevitable real obstacles to such relationships which produce "stink." And of course in the case of these two men the question—though basically the same one all human beings must confront—is burdened with the guilt David (not Giovanni) feels about homosexuality.

As for the truth in Giovanni's speech, throughout the novel David consistently detaches, withdraws from people, and the reason seems to be recurring distaste for the flesh. He eventually expresses repugnance for Hella, too, the girl for whom he has left Giovanni.

> I don't know, now, when I first looked at Hella and found her stale, found her body uninteresting, her presence grating. . . . I trace it to something as fleeting as the tip of her breast lightly touching my forearm as she leaned over me to serve my supper. I felt my flesh recoil. Her underclothes, drying in the bathroom, which I had often thought of as smelling even rather improbably sweet and as being washed much too often, now began to seem unaesthetic and unclean. . . . I sometimes watched her naked body move and wished that it were harder and firmer, I was fantastically intimidated by her breasts, and when I entered her I began to feel that I would never get out alive.

First of all, David is clearly revolted by what distinguishes Hella as a female—"the tip of her breast," her feminine underclothes, the softness of her woman's body. Or perhaps we should say, David is increasingly revolted by his intimacy with such a creature, since her continuing presence, serving him meals they take together, her laundry hanging in their bathroom, the movement of her naked body in the house they occupy, evidences their deepening intimacy. There is even an interesting hint that David recognizes and resists his tendency to idealize Hella (or a tendency in her to nurture such idealization), since it has once seemed to him that her underclothes smelled too sweet and were too clean—that is, he has occasionally felt a need to preserve the realities of the human body, even the "stink." Like Giovanni's speech, this passage suggests that David's sexual, or fleshly confusion is a front for emotional disability, since he exaggerates the case for, *or* against his lovers. Whether the sexual doubt or the emotional incapacity came first is difficult to say, but it seems probably that David *has* never loved anyone, as Giovanni asserts.

We can speculate, though, that David's emotional anesthesia (it would seem to be anesthesia, since his attractions are undoubtedly strong enough to involve him temporarily and to create conflict about his actions) is born of unconscious attitudes about some bad "stink" of love and of sex, attitudes which may have spoiled and distorted both the past and the present. Then, we can look at David's case as presented by Baldwin. For example, in the ending of *Giovanni's Room* Baldwin makes David sound like a "fallen hero." Or, as Arthur Miller has demonstrated with similar awareness of the modern, peculiarly American sexual/emotional dilemma in *After the Fall,* no one who remains "alive" after the experience of both psychic and real violence (the inner and the external "wars") can call himself innocent—we all acquire knowledge, and self-knowledge, whether we wish to or not: the aftermath is "after the fall." I think this is where we find (and leave) David at the end of *Giovanni's Room,* on the verge of compelling, possibly constructive self-knowledge. Like Quentin in *After the Fall,* David is seen locked in a narcissistic self (which we might correctly guess to be adolescent, according to the evidence provided from his past); that is, there may be a point in past time when David's "innocence" was first threatened by a knowledge of adult sexuality and adult love. In this final scene David stands before a mirror such as Giovanni has alluded to ("you love your mirror"), a mirror he is "terribly aware of." He sees his body trapped in this mirror "as it is trapped in time," and he murmurs about putting away childish things. Yet there is no resolution as David walks away from the house he has shared with Hella, and from France, pursued by the torn pieces of a note which informed him of Giovanni's execution.

David's past offers a fairly classic psychological background for his present: his father who attempted to be a "buddy" when David wanted instead the "merciful distance" of father and son; his dead mother, remembered as fragile yet somehow "dangerous"; and nervous, brittle Aunt Ellen, sharing their household, with her inconsistencies of vulgar cocktail flirtations and harsh judgments of her brother's social relations. The conflict and confused values of David's past are subsequently reflected, I think, in the inordinate threat he feels in Giovanni's room: more than the mere presence and possession of his lover, he fears a dark and emotionally debilitating chaos of himself which the room symbolizes. In particular, his experiences with Giovanni in that room must recollect that first sexual encounter with the boy Joey, and the anxiety accompanying it. So David is in a sense reliving his past in the immediacy of Giovanni's room. Baldwin here approaches a universality in his rendering in sea imagery of what seems dangerous and chaotic to David:

> . . . life in that room seemed to be occurring beneath the sea, time flowed past indifferently above us. . . . It became, in a way, every room I had ever been in and every room I find myself in hereafter will remind me of Giovanni's room. . . . Life in that room seemed to be occurring underwater, as I say, and it is certain that I underwent a sea-change there.

This is of course a description of feelings of unreality, or what is remote from the external world. At the same time, David's impressions of his life with Giovanni in that room imply a loss of self which ironically might be desirable rather than disturbing, were he at peace with himself; that is, the feeling of being "beneath the sea," of life occurring "underwater," and the diminished sense of time all plead for that loss of ego and momentary creation of an other, third entity which D. H. Lawrence, for one, believed essential to fullest union between human beings. The images also suggest a comfortable, floating prenatal state. There is more evidence that the two are enwombed in Giovanni's room: the room is literally dark—its windows have been painted over; and it is messy and cluttered, full of Giovanni's "regurgitated life." Yet this womb state becomes more and more intolerable for David.

To emphasize the universality of Baldwin's imagery here as strongly depicting a kind of sexual attraction which in early experiences often threatens, and which can later lead to homosexuality, or inordinate fear of homosexuality, or unreasonable fear of and distaste for females, I want to cite interesting brief examples from other writers who have used sea and water imagery similarly. Such imagery is of course standard in representing the sexual or the womblike, but there are particular instances where threat or downright seduction is felt by those responding. In Hart Crane's "Voyages," the first in the series concludes with these lines:

> oh brilliant kids, frisk with your dog. Fondle your shells and sticks, bleached By time and the elements; but there is a line You must not cross nor ever trust beyond it Spry cordage of your bodies to caresses Too lichen-faithful from too wide a breast. The bottom of the sea is cruel.

These images suggest threat, even seduction from a maternal force, unperceived by the innocent children but seen and spoken of from a vantage point of a somewhat fatalistic adulthood: They must not trust their bodies to the sea's "caresses/Too lichen-faithful from too wide a breast"; yet their exuberant and spontaneous play with a dog and with toys of "shells and sticks" may put them in danger. But the speaker's perception and advice seem absolute: "there is a line you must not cross" because, ultimately, "the bottom of the sea is cruel." If we approach interpretation symbolically, the shells and sticks the children "fondle" in play may be the male genitalia, innocent playthings in childhood but empowered emblems of adulthood as one matures. The sea, certainly maternal ("breast"), and comforting ("caresses"), suggests the first prenatal water in which one floated and that first powerful source of nourishment and care, one's mother. Yet there is danger in trusting the "cordage" of one's body (in remaining attached, in a figurative umbilical sense) to this comfort which comes from a breast "too wide" and "too lichen-faithful" (faithful, perhaps, to an earlier and more fundamental love—the father). Thus the urge to go "too far" in playing near the sea, while open to literal interpretation (or to being read as a "death-wish"), seems also to mean the strong attraction of unconscious incestuous impulses of a male towards his mother—this is the line one must not cross. And the finality of the last line—"the bottom of the sea is cruel"—implies that annihilation would result from following through such an urge. (The death-wish, incidentally, is a variation on the Oedipal desire to return to the womb.) This poet has perhaps dealt with personal incestuous impulses by sublimating them into art (though the poet in question was in fact homosexual); in real life, though, such attraction in its lingering destructive form usually maims or destroys adult heterosexual potential. And the speaker in this poem might be David, Yves, Eric, Rufus Scott from Baldwin's fiction.

In the last two stories of Hemingway's *In Our Time* (the "Big Two-Hearted River" stories) the watery threat is a swamp, or rather, the spot where a river famous for its fishing possibilities narrows into swamp. (Hemingway takes Nick Adams very seriously, so that it's hard to say whether or not he is punning on "fish," and fishing, in coarse allusion to the rumored pungency of the vaginal orifice.) In the final pages, Part II, Nick consciously avoids fishing any "deep holes" or approaching the swamp. His thoughts run, "It would not be possible to walk through a swamp like that. The branches grew so low . . . You could not crash through the branches." Entrance to the swamp where the river narrows is in fact blocked by a big cedar slanting across (a hymenal obstruction? more remotely, the threatening paternal phallus?), and Nick's thoughts again are that he "did not want to go in there now. He felt a reaction against deep wading with the water deepening up under his armpits. . . ." Indeed, Nick tells himself the fishing there would be "tragic," and Hemingway uses the episode to focus on his troubled state of mind, an emotional anesthesia which prevents him from admitting anything difficult or complicated to his present existence. In short it is implied Nick has had a nervous breakdown as a result of the violence, hate, war and gore experienced in the other stories of *In Our Time,* and the fishing trip is therapeutic. Nick's condition in these last stories is a signal of that psychic wound every Hemingway protagonist seems to incur; and though there are many causes and effects set in motion, one area of cause-and-effect is the Hemingway hero's relations with the opposite sex, often marked by suspicion, withdrawals (parallel to his periodic retreat in war), and reluctance for deep or permanent alliances. For example, in another story ("The End of Something") Nick disentangles himself from a girlfriend, Marjorie (though she is an excellent fishing partner!), fearing a confining permanent relation; in "Soldier's Home" Krebs, returned from war, cannot bring himself to an active interest in the young hometown girls who stroll past the porch of his parents' home; Mr. and Mrs. Elliot in a story so-titled drift into separate homosexual attachments essentially because their pre-marital conception of themselves was impossibly virginal and pure, and once married they consider that the prime purpose of sexual intercourse is to produce babies (the story repeatedly uses the line, "Mr. and Mrs. Elliot tried very hard to have a baby")—failing in this, and by implication in their sexual relations, they pretty much give up on the marriage. All of these Hemingway men (of whom Nick is prototypical), then, are eventually blocked from taking an active male role with women; in this, their psychic state seems very like that of Baldwin's male characters. Hemingway's swampy unknown is like the confusion of Giovanni's room, where life was taking place "beneath the sea," "occurring underwater." When the Davids run from such rooms they are running from the line they must not cross, or from the bottom of the sea—the threat of annihilation or non-existence—as much as from their male lovers. Incidentally, Hemingway's swamp imagery is rather specifically female genital, since the entrance to the swamp (vaginal orifice) is clustered with thickets and trees (pubic growth), whereas the threat of Giovanni's room for David is twofold, since in living there he is refusing an active male heterosexual role and he is assuming a female role with Giovanni (in the sense that Giovanni goes out to work and earn, David stays home to clean and cook).

In *Giovanni's Room* there is also more literal mention of the threat of women, as the two men talk. Again water is the metaphor. This discussion is found *between* the descriptions of Giovanni's room jointed and quoted above (between Chapters 1 and 2 of Part II). David has said to Giovanni, "You don't seem to have a very high opinion of women." He replies, "oh, women! Women are like water. They are tempting like that, and they can be that treacherous, and they can seem to be that bottomless, you know?" (This recalls the above images of Hart Crane and Hemingway. Oddly enough, it also parallels a speech of Lambert Strether in *The Ambassadors*—Strether, trying to comprehend the mystery and charm of Madame de Vionnet, remarks, "Women are endlessly absorbent. To deal with them is to walk on water.") David's reply to Giovanni, "that can be very lonely," is a reminder that Baldwin's protagonists always seem groping from an immense loneliness, carrying on an unarticulated search.

II

What they are fundamentally groping for is love. This search for love is established thematically in the first pages of *Another Country*, in the form of a question, "do you love me?" wailing from a saxophone. In asking the question, though, the Negro saxophonist (who seems to speak for the Baldwin characters in general) sweeps over past and present, distributing the question among those figures in the past—parents, parent-figures, even nations—whose loyalty and devotion are to be doubted. This man for example is putting the question rather aggressively to a great blurred white American audience whose "love" has been withheld. This audience is described as

> being assaulted by the saxophonist who perhaps no longer wanted their love and merely hurled his outrage at them with the same contemptuous, pagan pride with which he humped the air. And yet the question was terrible and real; the boy was blowing with his lungs and guts out of his own short past; somewhere in that past, in the gutters or gang fights or gang shags; in the acrid room, on the sperm-stiffened blanket, behind marijuana or the needle, under the smell of piss in the precinct basement, he had received the blow from which he never would recover and this no one wanted to believe.

This is the "rage of the disesteemed" (a phrase from *Notes of a Native Son*), glaring in the eyes of every black character in *Another Country*. Yet the issues are not only racial, though race has usually tipped the balance towards ruin, dealing the blows from which they never recover (like Rufus and Ida Scott). The issues extend to every man's personal fight for self-esteem (and therefore to the white characters in *Another Country*, too); and they are rooted in the sexual, just as the passage above is vivid with sexuality, in fact violent sexuality. The player "assaults," "hurls," "humps the air" (slang for the sexual act); there is violence between males (gang fights) and between males and females (gang shags); the aftermath of these acts hypothesized by Baldwin (acts which isolate, alienate, or at least provide escape) is unpleasant, in terms of sense response ("the sperm-stiffened blanket," "the smell of piss in the precinct basement"); the psychic response—the fatal "blow"—is left ambiguous—symbolic, as an accumulation of blows (like "the 400") yet possibly real, at the hands of an unseen policeman (who would also represent the authority of the unloving society). But this passage also suggests the pride of a child who has found its ideals betrayed ("contemptuous, pagan pride"), or its "mother" (America) faithless, and who then plunges into every sort of rebellious action intent on losing its innocence (or destroying itself) in the wake of the collapsed ideal. Indeed, *all* children must feel the "rage of the disesteemed" at least briefly, when they discover the frustrating truth that all their wants and needs are not always instantly filled: what happens after that discovery is our concern here.

I think Baldwin's characters ask two further questions which correspond to "do you love me?" *Will* "you" love me if and when I lose my innocence (this question is being forced in the behavior described from the saxophonist's past); and, conversely, can *I* love *you* when in my widening vision you appear corrupt or faithless? The "you" is any adult-parent-authority figure originally esteemed; the implicit issue is sexuality, and one's broadening experience of sexuality, first by observation, eventually by act (sometimes retaliatory, as the saxophonist's playing seems to be). Baldin stresses the importance of the past in answering such questions, especially absorbing the past into the present rather than fleeing from it, lest we all, in Fitzgerald's classic phrase, like "boats against the current," be "borne-back ceaselessly into the past." But his characters fear the past, and in his belief that "the past is all that makes the present coherent" (*Notes of a Native Son*) he often raises the stature of those (like Cass Silenski) who make a more successful effort at absorbing and comprehending it.

So many of Baldwin's people—David of *Giovanni's Room,* Rufus Scott and Vivaldo Moore in *Another Country*—flee from the past that the insights of an exception, Cass Silenski, are of interest. On the night of Rufus Scott's suicide, Cass had spoken urgently to him:

> When you're older you'll see, I think, that we all commit our crimes. The thing is not to lie about them—to try to understand what you have done, why you have done it. . . . That way, you can begin to forgive yourself. That's very important. If you don't forgive yourself you'll never be able to forgive anybody else and you'll go on committing the same crimes forever.

But Rufus is not able to "forgive" himself, and he commits suicide. (He is like Maggie in Miller's *After the Fall*: both are unable to confront their hatreds, and self-hatred, and thus to diminish their guilts.) Later, after Rufus's funeral, Cass watches Vivaldo undergo a self-examination (the funeral is a catalyst for several characters). "She listened because she knew that he was going back over it, looking at it, trying to put it all together, to understand it, to express it. But he had not expressed it. He had left something of himself back there on the streets of Brooklyn which he was afraid to look at again." What Vivaldo remembers but doesn't put into words is a vicious experience in which he and his buddies beat up a young homosexual, yet he can't look at the incident hard enough to understand why he participated in it. Cass rightly judges that "Vivaldo's recollections in no sense freed him from the things recalled. He had not gone back into it . . . he regarded it with a fascinated, even romantic horror, and he was looking for a way to deny it." Vivaldo, like the others, may go on "committing the same crimes forever." Cass may not; certainly in this scene she painfully recognizes some of her own secrets, or "crimes." And her recognition foreshadows later suffering, after the affair with Eric and the collapse of her marriage. Her thoughts precisely echo Baldwin's statement, "the past is all that makes the present coherent."

> Perhaps such secrets, the secrets of everyone, were only expressed when the person laboriously dragged them into the light of the world, imposed them on the world, and made them a part of the world's experience. Without this effort, the secret place was merely a dungeon in which the person perished . . . and she saw, with a dreadful reluctance, why this effort was so rare. Reluctantly, because she then realized that Richard had bitterly disappointed her by writing a book in which he did not believe. In that moment she knew, and she knew that Richard would never face it, that the book he had written to make money represented the absolute limit of his talent. It had not been written to make money—if only it had been! It had really been written because he was afraid, afraid of things dark, strange, dangerous, difficult, and deep.

Experience, then, means loss of innocence through, for one thing, seeing limitations as one faces realities. Such lost innocence is the general subject of most of *Another Country*, after Rufus Scott's funeral. People like Vivaldo and Cass plunge into chaos from the safety of their illusioned, childlike worlds. As Cass confesses to Eric, in their farewell rendezvous before a grotesque modern painting at the Museum of Modern Art, she had loved her husband like a child, "and now the bill for all that dreaming had come in." Tough Ida Scott, Rufus's sister, puts it more cynically: "You have to pay your dues." Youth and innocence go together; in the above scene, Eric watches Cass's face, "from which the youth was now, before his eyes, departing."

In a more economical and less romantic scene, Vivaldo discovers realities, possibly limitations, through Ida's confession of her infidelity. And he does take a step towards liberating self-knowledge when he pleads with her, "Please, Ida, whatever has to be done, to set us free—let's do it." Her reply, "let me finish my story," suggests that the process of bringing oneself up to date in reality in order to grow is a neverending one, which requires courage. (The ending of Edward Albee's *Who's Afraid of Virginia Woolf?* is like this, when George destroys the illusion of their child—the American Dream?—in a drastic move towards beginning again. "No, it's not certainty," for any of these troubled protagonists, as Arthur Miller has Quentin assert in the ending of *After the Fall*—and the spirit is the same in all these works—"but it does seem feasible not to be afraid.") So Ida goes on relating to Vivaldo how she prostituted herself literally and figuratively to escape from Harlem. The kitchen in which this scene occurs becomes invested with emotional realities, is "immortalized" in Vivaldo's mind.

> The coffee pot, now beginning to growl, was real, and the blue fire beneath it and the pork chops in the pan, and the milk which seemed to be turning sour in his belly. The coffee cups, as he thoughtfully washed them, were real, and the water which ran into them, over his heavy, long hands. Sugar and milk were real, and he set them on the table, another reality, and cigarettes were real and he lit one. Smoke poured from his nostrils and a detail that he needed for his novel, which he had been searching for for months, fell, neatly and vividly, like the tumblers of a lock, into place in his mind.

It is all "real" because Vivaldo is letting something really happen to him, something involving another person's separate life and emotions. What then happens, after Ida's revelations and Vivaldo's reaction to them, is "after the fall" in the sense of crucial yet painful awareness, for both. Vivaldo discovers from this scene the *tender* aspect of love; it is forced upon him through realization that his temporary revulsion for the erotic aspect of love, because he sees Ida for the moment as a whore, does not cancel out all his feelings for her. Here Vivaldo is more enlightened than David of *Giovanni's Room* though it hasn't yet become "feasible" for him not to be afraid. "Life is catching up with us," Eric tells him in the phone call interrupting this scene with Ida, meaning that such confrontations with ourselves and others are necessary to reveal deeper feelings. In the previously cited scene of Cass's introspection she discovered the real, and limited Richard, and regards it as her "crime," since it now hurts them both, that she formerly idealized him; in the same sense it will be Vivaldo's crime if he now hates Ida for spoiling his make-believe about her.

> He thought to himself that he had at last got what he wanted, the
> truth out of Ida, or the true Ida; and he did not know how he was
> going to live with it. . . . a wilderness of anger, pity, love, and con-
> tempt and lust all raged together in him. She, too, was a whore;
> how bitterly he had been betrayed!

At this moment Vivaldo experiences the "rage of the disesteemed,"
and his bitterness is exaggerated in its universality, with the weight
of past betrayals—"she, too, was a whore!"

If Ida, *too,* is a whore, in Vivaldo's somewhat self-pitying phrase,
who then was the first? The first seductress, the first woman whose
charms were paraded before one's awakening senses—surely, it is
one's mother. We go back to the spectre of David's mother, in *Giovanni's Room.*

> My mother had been carried to the graveyard when I was five. I
> scarcely remember her at all, yet she figured in my nightmares, blind
> with worms, her hair as dry as metal and brittle as a twig, straining
> to press me against her body; that body so putrescent, so sickening
> soft, that it opened, as I clawed and cried, into a breach so enormous
> as to swallow me alive.

Fear and guilt keynote this terrifying fusion of sex and death in the
boy's memory. It is hard to tell which came first in his fantasies, the
mother's death or his fatal attachment and attraction to her. Yet
other characters record similar responses. Vivaldo says to Eric, "Did
you ever feel you were being eaten alive by a woman?" Rufus Scott
declares Leona's insatiability. It is a cannibalistic threat of annihilation, in fact a none-too-surprising reversal in these men of an infantile "cannibalistic" urge to swallow up or eat alive (to possess)
that major source of sustenance, the mother. In the passage below,
David's fears approach a wish for self-annihilation because of un-
worthiness, as his dead mother watches them all from her photograph,

> a pale, blonde woman, delicately put together, dark-eyed, and
> straight-browed, with a nervous, gentle mouth. But something about
> the way the eyes were set in the head and stared straight out, some-
> thing very faintly sardonic and knowing in the set of the mouth
> suggested that, somewhere beneath this tense fragility was a strength
> as various as it was unyielding and, like my father's wrath, dangerous
> because it was so entirely unexpected. My father rarely spoke of her
> and when he did he covered, by some mysterious means, his face; he
> spoke of her only as my mother and, in fact, as he spoke of her, he

might have been speaking of his own. Ellen spoke of my mother often, saying what a remarkable woman she had been but she made me uncomfortable. I felt that I had no right to be the son of such a mother.

The passage shows that David's mother has become idealized, apparently by all parties, even though in point of fact she must have been in a somewhat more real relationship with them during her life, especially with his father, at least in terms of a sexual act which produced their son. Also, she emerges as a figure of fragile but unyielding strength, and as "remarkable." It is hardly surprising that David felt unworthy of her. David's mother haunts him, attracts him, yet is "unyielding,"—to him, at least. There is a comparable situation in Book II of *Another Country*, in a discussion of Yves' mother, when it has been decided that Yves will follow Eric, his lover, to New York in a few months. Yves exclaims, "I suppose I must go and visit my whore of a mother and tell her that she will never see me any more." There is affection in Yves' "must," as well as a half-conscious urge to test her affection with the fact of his departure. He then relates his mother's amours during the German occupation of France during World War II, when he was five (David, too, of *Giovanni's Room*, "lost" his mother when five). Yves seems to feel, bitterly, that his mother took on the French problems of German occupation a little too singlehandedly, one German soldier after another, in the bistro where she worked and which she now owns: he implies that in buying their future she sold herself. Yves, who has of course become a whore himself (he is a male prostitute), now visits her bistro periodically, on which occasions they enact an ironic communion of drinking together. She offers him cognac, he always accepts, demanding a double, then they drink to each other's health. Sometimes he toasts, *"A nos amours,"* and she replies, *"A nos amours."* Yves has been disappointed (betrayed, deserted) by his mother in life as David was by his in her death, yet both men retain half-fascinated, half-revolted attachments to the maternal figure—they retain an intimacy, one might say.

This fascination and revulsion—or, intimacy—felt by David, Yves, Eric, Vivaldo (and Baldwin's male characters are almost monotonously similar) for women, rooted perhaps in early experiences with mothers or mother-figures now fixed in the memory, seems to be the psychic fact behind their tendency to hold themselves "virginal" or, at the other extreme, to prostitute themselves for their own sex. In either case they are avoiding commitment to a legitimate heterosexual position. David for example finds Hella repulsive when faced with legalizing his relations with her into marriage; we can speculate that his affair with her has been sustained on the basis of a certain lawlessness, and to make their union lawful would bring her dangerously nearer the category occupied in his unconscious by the idealized and threatening mother, himself dangerously nearer unadmitted incestuous impulses and ambivalent feelings. The alternative for these men, which seems at first safer, is flight into the arms of men. Yves and Eric are seen debating this alternative too. A few speeches *after* Yves' anecdote about his mother and himself, and their *"a nos amours,"* Yves declares his love for Eric: *"Je t'aime bien."* Yves seems to be choosing the more dependable love object, in Eric; though Eric's response is more doubtful—he ponders and desires this "love," yet is unable to express any of his own feelings about their relationship. (And Eric is, after all, leaving Yves and Europe.)

III

It was offered earlier that the question aggressively put to the great parental audience by the saxophonist in *Another Country* ("do you love me?") really involves several questions, of loss of innocence and threatened loss of love ("can you love me?" "will I love you?"). The young man in discovery of his own sexuality (David, for example, in relation to his adults) is led to examine his idealized people in a new light as part of the attempt to know himself. As the answers almost always seem at first confusing so the judgments may be extreme: either his own flesh is vile, or the purity of the ideal must be sacrificed. In such a scheme of absolutes, "mothers" may become "whores." This is Yves' response, or David's suspicion of his Aunt Ellen. The other feeling, of one's own corrupted flesh, is well depicted in the situation of John Grimes in *Go Tell It on the Mountain,* which opens on the morning of his 14th birthday. On this morning John lies in bed later than usual, pondering his "sin" of masturbation in the school lavatory, imagining a woman's nakedness in the cracked walls of his bedroom, and reflecting on his curious discovery of an "identity" though the "eye altogether alien and impersonal" of a teacher who once told him he was bright: in all this "he began to perceive, in wild uneasiness, his individual existence." These thoughts carry over to a scene in the kitchen, as he watches his mother working, where "dirt"—real dirt of the apartment and the city—stands for the "filth" of his own mind.

> The room was narrow and dirty; nothing could alter its dimensions, no labor could ever make it clean. Dirt was in the walls and the floorboards . . . was in the fine ridges of the pots and pans, scoured daily . . . was in every corner, angle, crevice of the monstrous stove. . . . John thought with shame and horror, yet in angry hardness of heart: *He who is filthy, let him be filthy still.* Then he looked at his mother, seeing, as though she were someone else, the dark, hard lines running downward from her eyes, and the deep, perpetual scowl in her forehead . . . was it not he, in his false pride and his evil imagination, who was filthy? Through the storm of tears that did not reach his eyes, he stared at the yellow room; and the room shifted, the light of the sun darkened, and his mother's face changed. Her face became the face that he gave her in his dreams, the face that had been hers in a photograph he had seen once, long ago, a photograph taken before he was born. This face was young and proud, uplifted, with a smile that made the wide mouth beautiful and glowed in the enormous eyes. It was the face of a girl who knew that no evil could undo her, and who could laugh, surely, as his mother did not laugh now. Between the two faces there stretched a darkness and a mystery that John feared, and that sometimes caused him to hate her.

John has no guarantee, in the helpless egocentricity of youth, that he himself has not in some mysterious way caused the "hardening" of his mother from that era of the photograph, before his birth. So he sometimes hates himself, for his "evil" imaginings (and John, whose father is a minister, has been much influenced and pressured by evangelical Christianity), and sometimes he hates his mother, for some unspecified knowledge of life which has spoiled her girlishness. Either way, though, sexuality is the underlying current of John's imaginings. He is aroused to fear and hatred by a "darkness and a mystery" which stretches between past and present in the two faces of his mother; in other words, that period surrounding his conception, birth and infancy is an unknown to him, yet something he has half-consciously speculated about. Implicit in such imaginings, since concurrent with his own sexual awakening, would be that sexual activity between his parents which of course at some point produced him; and it bothers John that in the photo "taken before he was born" his mother is laughing and young and proud, so that the "evil" which "undid" her seems connected with himself (or with his father, of course, an obvious alternative not directly developed in this scene, although John certainly shows hatred for his father). We can go a step further and cite the interesting paradox in the incestuous impulse seen in a character like John: part of the unconscious wish to take the father's place sexually with the mother, rooted in physical attraction and emotional attachment to her (both essentially helpless emotions at this stage) is a cherished unconscious belief in two impossibilities—participation in the sex act which resulted in his own conception, yet *preservation* of the supposed innocence or sexual purity of the idealized mother (and therefore, being a "better" man than his father), "the face that he gave her in his dreams." Of course, if and when John Grimes frees himself from the helplessness of the attraction and attachment now stirring in him in adolescence, he will be on the way to his independence and male adulthood.

Another example of the notion of one's corrupt flesh, and the unconscious conviction, which seems fatal in Baldwin's fiction to heterosexual relations or commitments to lawful wedlock, that there are only mothers *or* whores (the ideal or the shattered ideal), is seen in Vivaldo Moore's relations with a girl named Jane. The commentator, significantly, is Rufus Scott, who loves Vivaldo and is possessive of him. Rufus professes not to understand why Vivaldo continues his affair with Jane, who is sloppy and tends to behave like a drunken, promiscuous slut; yet Rufus uses this very fact as evidence for a curious but reasonable conclusion about Vivaldo's emotions, as a proof that Vivaldo will never "betray" (desert) him: "Even his affair with Jane was evidence in his favor, for if he were really likely to betray his friend for a woman, as most white men seemed to do, especially if the friend were black, then he would have found himself a smoother chick, with the manners of a lady and the soul of a whore." In projecting a "smoother chick" who might be more threatening competition for Vivaldo's love, Rufus knows more intuitively about the realities of relations between the sexes than he himself can ever act upon. Though the woman Rufus hypothesizes is still split in two parts—the ideal (lady) and the shattered ideal (whore)—he is on the right track. His remarks echo more professional opinion about healthy love between the sexes: "Whoever is to be really free and happy in love must have overcome his deference for women and come to terms with the idea of incest with the mother or sister." Coming to terms requires a second stage: "To ensure a fully normal attitude in love, two currents of feeling have to unite . . . the tender affectionate feelings and the sensual feelings." (Freud, *Sexuality and the Psychology of Love*) But none of the characters here discussed can come to such terms, so that for them reality must always "stink" of disappointed idealism and unworthy, corrupted physicality—there is no lasting fusion of the tender and the sensual.

IV

I think David speaks for most Baldwin protagonists in the first pages of *Giovanni's Room*. "Perhaps, as we say in America, I wanted to find myself. This is an interesting phrase, not current as far as I know in the language of any other people, which certainly does not mean what it says but betrays a nagging suspicion that something has been misplaced." In Baldwin's fiction what has often been misplaced is one's healthy sexuality (for the sexuality of his males cannot be viewed as healthy as long as they are troubled about it). In a broader sense, his protagonists hardly ever arrive at a "healthy" reality but rather effect a "truce with reality" (a phrase used in *Notes of a Native Son*, in the context of being born Negro in America), which Baldwin says is "all one can hope for." For his characters personally this truce is often homosexuality, but a homosexuality which leaves something unresolved. In fact, to resort to professional statement again, it sounds like David and the other males discussed progress through a first stage of self-analysis and awareness approximating that stage in formal psycho-analysis, but they do not go on to shed outdated responses or alter behavior. The process described below fits the situation in such a novel as *Another Country*.

> In quite a number of cases the analysis divides itself into two clearly distinguishable stages: in the first, the physician procures from the patient the necessary information, makes him familiar with the premises and postulates of psychoanalysis, and unfolds to him the reconstruction of the genesis of his disorder as deduced from the material brought up in the analysis. In the second stage the patient himself lays hold of the material put before him, works on it, recollects what he can of the apparently repressed memories, and behaves as if he were living the rest over again. . . . It is only during this work that he experiences, through overcoming resistances, the inner

change aimed at, and acquires for himself the convictions that make
him independent of the physician's authority. . . . One may insti-
tute a comparison with two stages of a journey. The first comprises
all the necessary preparations. . . . One then has the right, and the
possibility, of travelling into a distant country, but after all these
preliminary exertions one is not yet there. . . . For this to happen
one has to make the journey itself from one station to the other, and
this part of the performance may well be compared with the second
stage in the analysis. (Freud, "A Case of Homosexuality in a
Woman")

Baldwin's characters seldom "lay hold of the material" enough to
make the journey to another country. Their self-knowledge remains
too cynical and clinging to a disappointed idealism. The reader for
example shares Vivaldo's quick insight, after the act of intercourse
with Eric, that he is "condemned to women"; and we move with
him from that incident to Ida's revelations which illuminate his
relations with her. Beyond that, though, we see only that Vivaldo
"did not know how he was going to live with it" (the shattered
ideal) as he pleads with her, "Bear with me, please give me a little
time." Vivaldo has travelled farther than David, whom we leave
in a reflection much like John Grimes' distress on his 14th birthday
about his corrupt flesh; David says, "I move at last from the mirror
and begin to cover that nakedness which I must hold sacred, though
it be never so vile." David is still a split person too, and doesn't
understand what reality is. Nor do those characters who talk tough,
like Ida Scott, seem to improve their happiness. In answer to Cass's
crucial question, "what does one replace a dream with?" Ida says,
"with reality." But she goes on to betray her own disappointed and
unresolved idealism: "What you people don't know is that life is a
bitch, baby. It's the biggest hype going." This split over the ideal is
Baldwin's predominant position. We leave his characters on the
threshold of the second stage of self-knowledge, ready but unable to
begin their journey to another and better country of themselves.

V

But Baldwin still believes in love, equating it with "grace," as
both means and end of greater human understanding. He makes
some positive statements about love in his essays. In *The Fire Next
Time,* in national and personal terms, he strikes at the necessity for

coming to terms with outdated idealism, asserting that Americans chronically do not wish to face reality, though the American dream stands to be revised in harsher light. For as long as they resist such change they will lack "authority" (just as the men in his fiction lack authority). "It is the responsibility of free men to trust and to celebrate what is constant—birth, struggle, and death are constant, and so is love, though we may not always think so—and to apprehend the nature of change, to be able and willing to change. I speak of change not on the surface but in the depths—change in the sense of renewal." But one must comprehend love as something more than childish ideal and demand. He discusses a kind of love that is "so desperately sought and so cunningly avoided. Love takes off the masks that we fear we cannot live without and know we cannot live within. I use the word 'love' here not merely in the personal sense but as a state of being, or a state of grace—not in the infantile American sense of being made happy but in the tough and universal sense of quest and daring and growth."

This conception of "love" is furthered in another passage from *The Fire Next Time,* on the topic of sensuality, so that it resembles that union of tender affectionate feelings and sensual feelings prescribed above. "To be sensual is to respect and rejoice in the force of life, of life itself, and to be *present* in all that one does, from the effort of loving to the breaking of bread." Such sensuality is more than lasciviousness, or panting ungratified sexuality—"The word 'sensual' is not intended to bring to mind quivering dusky maidens or priapic black studs." Leaving aside racial implications (a special aspect of the problem), we see it is still a state of "grace" or renewal being described ("to celebrate," and "the breaking of bread," after all, suggest "holy" communion). That Baldwin feels impelled to explore (in writing which postdates the fiction considered here) what sensuality is *not* is reminiscent of the troubled sexuality of his male characters, which is to say that Baldwin comprehends solutions that his characters do not enact, that he envisions a state in which men *co-exist* harmoniously with women who are neither "mothers" nor "whores," rather than cling to their convictions of desertions and betrayals from the opposite sex in perpetual self-justification of their own flights from and faithlessness towards them: this is a state in which reality would no longer "stink."

James Baldwin: At Ease in Apocalypse

by Irving Howe

At least in our literature, the black man remains invisible. Almost anyone can rage about "the Negro question," almost anyone pronounce and exhort. But only two or three American novelists have thus far managed to write novels in which Negro men and women come through as credible figures. How disconcerting it is, how unsettling to our liberal pieties, that only from William Faulkner, a Southerner whose opinions on this matter ranged from the benighted to the befuddled, have we gotten a sizable group of Negro characters in whose reality we can immediately believe! Why blacks should be invisible to white writers we have no difficulty in supposing ourselves to know, usually through a masochistic notion that does little credit to the humanity of either color. But what is a good deal more baffling is the scarcity of serious fiction by Negro writers. There is Richard Wright's *Native Son* and, still more notable, Ralph Ellison's *Invisible Man*; there are a few younger Negro writers of talent though not yet fulfillment; and not much else.

A few decades ago we all thought we knew why Negro writers were blocked. They were castrated by the psychology of deference; they kept their anger bottled up; they had not achieved that identity which comes to the suppressed only through rebellion. Then Richard Wright published *Native Son*, a crude but overwhelming book, in which the central figure is not so much a distinctive human being as an elemental force through which to release the rage black men had not dared to express. Other Negro writers, stirred and perhaps liberated by Wright's achievement, tried to imitate his posture of wrath, but rarely with success; for as it turned out, the significance of *Native Son*, which I take to be a major American text,

"James Baldwin: At Ease in Apocalypse" by Irving Howe. From *Harper's Magazine*, 237, no. 1420 (September, 1968), 92, 95–100. Copyright © 1968, by Minneapolis Star and Tribune Co., Inc. Reprinted from the September, 1968 issue of *Harper's Magazine* by permission of the author.

is at least partly that among books of its kind it was the one that came first.

In time, then, it began to seem that anger might not be enough and that protest might turn out to be a sterile box in which the middle-class whites, murmuring their guilt and sympathy, would be delighted to keep Negro writers locked. A young and then unknown black writer named James Baldwin wrote in 1951 that the failure of the protest novel "lies in its insistence that it is [man's] categorization alone which is real and which cannot be transcended." Rebelling against Richard Wright even while acknowledging that Wright had influenced him profoundly, Baldwin declared his wish to compose novels in which *the* Negro would be dissolved as a social phantom of hatred-and-condescension, and instead a variety of Negroes, in all their particularity and complexity, would be imagined. He wanted to write the kind of novel that would show the life of the Negroes through "an unspoken recognition of shared experiences which creates a way of life." And meanwhile he published those brilliant, nervous essays—gestures of repudiation, glimmers of intention —called *Notes of a Native Son.*

The program was Baldwin's, yet by a bitterly ironic turn, its realization came not from him but from another writer, Ralph Ellison, whose *Invisible Man* is the only novel written by an American Negro which on a major scale brings to imaginative life the experience of black people, both in the North and the South. Baldwin did publish *Go Tell It on the Mountain,* a delicate narrative, blending memoir and fiction, about his Harlem boyhood; but his major talent, then as now, was for the essay, first through a style of Jamesian elegance and later through a style of flaming declamation. Yet the program which the young Baldwin set for himself—a program of aesthetic autonomy and faithfulness to private experience, as against ideological noise and blunt stereotype—was almost impossible for the Negro writer to realize. Even *Invisible Man,* for all its imaginative freedom, could not do so completely.

In the early 'sixties there took place a fierce polemic between Ralph Ellison and myself concerning the role of the Negro writer in America, and more particularly, the extent to which that writer would have to accept the voicing of protest as his unavoidable obligation or burden. In the eyes of most literary people, Ellison had the better of this exchange. He seemed to be defending the independence of the creative act and the right of Negroes to compose with precisely the freedom white novelists enjoyed, while I seemed to be saying that for the foreseeable future the Negro writers would not be able, even if they wished, to escape the imperatives of pro-test. There is no point in rehearsing this argument here, and I am hardly the one to do it—except to remark that in those years the intellectual atmosphere, strongly conservative and antipolitical, predisposed many people to sympathize with Ellison's views, while today both of us would be denounced as "finks" by militant blacks and certain literary people for whom a nuance of thought looms as a personal affront.

When Baldwin published his novel *Another Country* in 1962, I saw it as a partial confirmation of my views. All of his earlier values —complexity, subtlety, irony—were abandoned in behalf of a style that was sometimes as crude, though never as powerful, as that of Wright in *Native Son*. For *Another Country* came out at a time when the Negro revolt was beginning to gather strength, and Bald-win, who had been one of its most eloquent public spokesmen, probably could not have avoided the stance of militancy even if he had cared to—the very stance which in his early essays he had found so damaging to literary achievement.

Now, after having read Baldwin's new novel *Tell Me How Long the Train's Been Gone*, I have come to feel that the whole prob-lem of Negro writing in America is far more complex than I had ever recognized, probably more complex than even Ellison had supposed, and perhaps so complex as to be, at this moment, almost beyond discussion. *Tell Me How Long the Train's Been Gone* is a remarkably bad novel, signaling the collapse of a writer of some dis-tinction. But apart from its intrinsic qualities, it helps make clear that neither militancy nor its refusal, neither a program of aesthetic autonomy nor its denial, seems enough for the Negro novelist who wishes to transmute the life of his people into a serious piece of fic-tion. No program, no rhetoric, no political position makes that much difference. What does make the difference I would now be hard pressed to say, but as I have been thinking about the Negro writers I know or have read, I have come to believe that their prob-lems are a good deal more personal than we have usually supposed. For the Negro writer, if he is indeed to be a *writer*, public posture matters less than personal identity. His problem is to reach into his true feelings, be they militant or passive, as distinct from the feel-ings he thinks he should have, or finds it fashionable to have, about the life of his fellow blacks. The Negro writer shares in the sufferings of an exploited race, and it would be outrageous to suppose that simply by decision he can avoid declaring his outrage; but he is also a solitary man, solitary insofar as he is a writer, solitary even more because he is a black writer, and solitary most of all if he is a black man who writes. Frequently he is detached from and in opposition to other blacks; unavoidably he must find himself troubled by his relationship to the whole looming tradition of Western literature, which is both his and never entirely his; and sooner or later he must profoundly wish to get away from racial polemic and dialectic, simply in order to reach, in his own lifetime, some completeness of being. As it seems to me, James Baldwin has come to a point where all of these problems crush down upon him and he does not quite know who he is, as writer, celebrity, or black man; so that he now suffers from the most disastrous of psychic conditions—a separation between his feelings and his voice.

II

The protagonist of Baldwin's new novel is named Leo Proudhammer, and thereby is announced a program of sorts. Leo: lion, king of the cats. Proudhammer: the black man's pride affirmed as if with a hammer.

Proudhammer is a successful Negro actor in his middle years; he enjoys the adulation of both other blacks and the white middle-class public; he is sharp in tongue, cultivated in speech, but puny in body. No one will miss the likelihood that Leo Proudhammer is at least in part an imaginative version of James Baldwin. The mixture of self-caress and feline scratching with which Proudhammer is treated strengthens the impression that we are in the presence of a narcissistic image.

At the outset Proudhammer suffers a severe heart attack. He has been working too hard, driving himself toward a status that brings no peace, tearing at his psyche with the claws of ambition. He is a great success; but still black. He is the long-time lover of Barbara, a distinguished white actress; but also drawn to homosexual affairs, especially with a young black militant named Christopher who offers release from the multiple hang-up, as Baldwin conceives it, of rationality and the stable psyche.

Proudhammer lies recuperating in a hospital while Barbara and

Christopher hover over him protectively. In abrupt flashes, he thinks back to the main events of his life, purring over and despising himself at the same time. The technique is not exactly a stunning innovation, but no matter: it has been serviceable in the past and could be again.

In one of the few persuasive portions of the novel, Leo's mind races back to the harshness of his boyhood in Harlem. There are echoes of *Go Tell It on the Mountain*: a grandiose, embittered, and weak father, his mind stocked with fantasies about old black kings even as he works at a wretched job in the garment center; a light-skinned warm mother, forever a haven; and Caleb, the older brother whom Leo loves and perhaps the only person he really can love. As a novelist, Baldwin has always been helpless before the mysteries of heterosexual love, and when he turns to homosexual love he usually drops into a whipped-cream sentimentalism which reminds one of nothing so much as the boy-meets-girl stories in the *Saturday Evening Post* of twenty years ago. The single strong and authentic affection he can dramatize is that between brothers, trapped together in a slum, despairing of their parents and the world, drawn into a web of incestuous defense.

James Baldwin can never be wholly uninteresting when he writes about Harlem, especially Harlem as seen through the eyes of a vulnerable black boy. This is the place he knows, the turf of his imagination. The boy Leo gets lost on a subway and is brought home, with an amused sardonic protectiveness, by a black stranger —an incident in which the quiet reality of racial bonds is shown far more convincingly than in scenes of screeching militancy. And the book is also alive whenever young Caleb and little Leo are together, learning to deceive their parents, discovering the threats and pleasures of the street, educating one another about the world that awaits them.

Yet even when he turns back to Harlem, Baldwin has become a slack and self-indulgent writer. Too frequently he falls back upon his worst fault: a lazy readiness to turn on his passionate rhetoric instead of building toward concrete presentation. It is a fault which leads him to falseness of characterization, a kind of indifference to the terms of his own imaginative creation.

One night Leo and Caleb are stopped by a vicious white police-man and painfully humiliated. That such incidents are all too common in our cities I do not doubt. Here is what Baldwin makes of it:

Caleb took out his wallet and handed it over. I could see that his hands were trembling. I watched the white faces. I memorized each mole, scar, pimple, nostril hair; I memorized the eyes, the contemptuous eyes. I wished I were God. And then I hated God.

Negro boys have plenty of reason to hate white cops. The first four of Baldwin's sentences, while not especially vivid, are credible. But let us remember that we are being shown a little boy, still rather innocent and strongly protected by his family. Can we then believe that at this frightening moment he would wish he were God? I greatly doubt it, yet must suppose it barely possible. What seems to me beyond credence, and a false intrusion by a writer imposing his own attitudes and thereby destroying the unity of his characterization, is the claim of the final sentence that the boy then hates God. Such a sentiment would be entirely persuasive in a grown-up Negro, especially the grown-up Negro who has written this novel; it might just barely be persuasive in the mind of the boy when *remembering* his humiliation. But no amount of sympathy can persuade one that in such a passage Baldwin is really portraying the experience of a Negro boy rather than making an oration about it.

A page or two later Leo asks Caleb:

> "Caleb," I asked, "are white people people?"
> "What are you talking about?"
> "I mean—are white people—*people?* People like us?"
> He looked down at me. His face was very strange and sad. It was a face I had never seen before. We climbed a few more stairs, very slowly. Then, "All I can tell you, Leo, is—well, *they* don't think they are."

Intrinsically, this passage seems false through an excess of cuteness: it fails to ring true not because we doubt that Leo should here be full of distress, but because we doubt that the boy would express himself in a way at once so convenient to both middle-class notions about childhood charm and Black Nationalist notions about them white devils. Worse still, even if the two passages I have just quoted are each independently persuasive, they utterly destroy one another in juxtaposition: for who can suppose that a boy sophisticated enough to have learned to "hate God" can a few pages later be innocent enough to wonder whether whites are "people"?

A linked falseness of language betraying sloppiness of feeling and

observation then appears in magnified form when the elder Proudhammer learns about his sons' humiliation:

> . . . his lips became bitter and his eyes grew dull. It was as though,
> after indescribable, nearly mortal effort, after grim years of fasting
> and prayer, after the loss of all he had, and after having been prom-
> ised by the Almighty that he had paid the price and no more would
> be demanded of his soul, which was harbored now: it was as though
> in the midst of his joyful feasting and dancing, crowned and robed,
> a messenger arrived to tell him a great error had been made, and
> that it was all to be done again. Before his eyes, then, the banquet
> and the banquet wines and the banquet guests departed, the robe
> and crown were lifted, and he was alone then, frozen out of his
> dream. . . .

This passage moves from an adequate, though by no means distinguished, description of the father's grief to a piece of willed fancy
which solicits our attention not for the character's feelings but for
Baldwin's verbal bravado. Without clarity or charm or firm relation between object and word, it is a speechmaker's prose.

III

Language rarely lies. It can reveal the insincerity of a writer's
claims simply through a grating adjective or an inflated phrase. We
come upon a frenzy of words and suspect it hides a paucity of feeling. In his new book Baldwin rarely settles into that controlled
exactness of diction which shows the writer to have focused on the
matter he wishes to describe or evoke; for Baldwin is now a writer
systematically deceiving himself through rhetorical inflation and
hysteria, whipping himself into postures of militancy and declara-
tions of racial metaphysics which—for him, in *this* book—seem utterly inauthentic.

One sign, a minor sign, of these troubles is Baldwin's compulsive
use of obscenity: those blazing terms of revelation, "shit" and
"fuck," occur endlessly in his dialogue. If it be said that this is the
way people really talk and that Baldwin is merely recording the
truth, I would reply that the defense is incompetent. Real-life conversation is notoriously imprecise, wasteful, and boring; no novelist,
even if he clings to a program of naturalistic fidelity, can avoid the
need to compress and stylize his dialogue; and Baldwin employs
these obscenities—they come to seem as emotionally affecting as

punctuation—for reasons that have nothing to do with literary realism. He is driven, in this book, by a need to show himself as a very up-to-the-minute swinger, a real tough guy, even though his native talent is for delicacy and nuance; he is writing with an eye toward that harlot called *Zeitgeist*.

A much more important sign of difficulty is the abandon with which Baldwin opens wide the spigot of his rhetoric, that astonishing flow of high eloquence which served him so well in his later essays but is a style almost certain to entrap a novelist. For if you sound like the voice of doom, an avenging god proclaiming the fire next time, then you don't really have to bother yourself with the small business of the novelist, which is to convey how other, if imaginary, people talk and act. Baldwin seems to have lost respect for the novel as a form, and his great facility with language serves only to ease his violations of literary strictness.

There is still a third way in which Baldwin's language betrays him, perhaps most fundamentally of all. When he writes about Proudhammer's rise to fame and the adulation he receives from friends and public, Baldwin slips into the clichés of soap opera, for which he had already shown an alarming fondness in the past when dealing with homosexual love. Buried deep within this seemingly iconoclastic writer is a very conventional sensibility, perfectly attuned to the daydream of success. Now, if you add all these styles together, you get a weird mixture: the prose of *Redbook* (the magazine for young mamas) and the prose of *Evergreen Review* (the magazine for all them mothers).

One series of flashbacks in *Tell Me How Long the Train's Been Gone* is concerned with Proudhammer's success as an actor, and the other series with Baldwin's notions about homosexual love as it is linked to black militancy. The first comes straight out of those movies of twenty-five years ago about the theatrical success of a poor slum urchin (call me Gershwin), shown now in his ripe old age at a testimonial dinner and looking back on his hard but honest climb to the top. The second tries out the idea that black men devoted to homosexuality and visions of racial apocalypse are somehow more pure, more soulful, and more trustworthy than men still messing around with women.

Proudhammer working as an odd-job boy at the summer theater of a nasty Jewish director; Proudhammer making his successful if nerve-racking debut in a little theater; Proudhammer as the idol of thousands; Proudhammer surrounded by his faithful growling valet, his long-suffering white lady lover, and his scrappy young black boyfriend (why must the fantasies of black writers be as mediocre as those of whites? because we are all, young Leo Proudhammer to the contrary notwithstanding, made of common clay)—all this comes straight from the heart and bowels of American mass culture.

Here is Leo Proudhammer, veteran of stage and screen, in a moment of reflection:

> There really is a kind of fellowship among people in the theater and I've never seen it anywhere else, except among jazz musicians. Our relationships are not peaceful and they certainly are not static, but in a curious way, they're steady. I think it may be partly because we're forced, in spite of the preposterous airs we very often give ourselves, to level with each other. . . .

A perfect speech, some time back, for Spencer Tracy; a perfect speech, a little time ahead, for Sidney Poitier. And then this bit on his first night:

> I've done lots of plays since then, some of them far more successful, but I'll never forget this one. There is nothing like the first plunge, and any survivor will tell you that. When the curtain came up, I knew I was going to vomit, right there. . . . The moment I delivered my first line, "No, Miss," I knew I was going to be all right. . . . I played that scene for all that was in it, for all that was in me, and for all the colored kids in the audience. . . .

Times change, of course. In my day the speaker of such lines would have been playing his heart out for a weeping Jewish mama.

This kind of junk, precisely because it is so familiar, indeed so deeply ingrained in our popular culture, may be judged fairly harmless. But Baldwin doesn't stop there. To the clichés of the ages he adds the cant of the moment. He writes on the tacit assumption that the guilt of his white liberal readers will allow him to say just about anything, indeed, that this audience will accept and revel in the tokens of his contempt, even if the price he must pay is a kind of literary suicide.

Here is Leo Proudhammer at the summer theater, with a rather decent white actress who has taken him to her bed, and taken him, so far as we can learn from Baldwin, not because he is black but simply because she thinks it might be fun:

> I worked with my lips and my tongue and my fingers, she wasn't working much yet, but she would; we fooled around. I can't say what was driving me. Perhaps I had to know—to know—*if* my body could be despised, how *much* it could be despised; perhaps I had to know how much was demanded of my body to make the shameful sentence valid. . . . I got her nearly naked on that sofa, shoes and stockings off, dress half on, half off, panties and bra on the floor. I was striding through a meadow, and it certainly felt like mine.

Brushing aside the dime store poetry of that last sentence, let us try to see what is happening here. The white actress, remember, has shown no hostility toward Leo; nothing preceding this passage indicates that he regards their encounter as warranting its "elevation" to a fateful meeting of colors; indeed, it has all been shown in terms of a casual excitement, a bit of fun; but Baldwin, in his presumption that his novel will be deepened and his audience shaken by the injection of racial shame, must transform the business of making an attractive white actress into a quasi-apocalyptic stroke of symbolism. And what enables him almost to get away with it is our presumption, reasonable enough in general, that a sexual meeting between people of different colors may indeed carry a large weight of meaning and trouble for at least one of them—a presumption which a careless and contemptuous writer can then fall back on to avoid the task of specific depiction and particular validation.

A similar falseness occurs during the summer theater experience. Proudhammer learns that "many of the roles played by white people could only be played by means of tricks, tricks which could never help one come closer to life, and all of which one would have to discard in order to play even one scene from, say, Ibsen."

Fair enough; even though this would also seem to be true for actors of any color. But then comes a wild leap of conclusion:

> I was discovering what some American blacks must discover: that the people who destroyed my history had also destroyed their own.

The inconsequence here is staggering. Is Proudhammer-Baldwin trying to say that white actors, having "destroyed their history," are as a group incapable of playing Ibsen? Or that there is some deep connection between the "destruction" of black history and the incapacity of most actors, white or black, to perform Ibsen? Or is he saying anything at all? The rhetoric becomes more and more oppressive and pretentious. Here is a Proudhammer reverie on the nature of love:

> Everyone wishes to be loved, but in the event, nearly no one can bear it. Everyone desires love but also finds it impossible to believe that he deserves it. However great the private disasters to which love may lead, love itself is strikingly and mysteriously impersonal; it is a reality which is not altered by anything one does.

And here is the way Baldwin supposes two grown-up people (not Greer Garson and Leslie Howard) to be talking to one another while the man lies sick in a hospital bed:

> ". . . Leo, you always want people to forgive *you*. But we, we others, we need forgiveness, too. We sometimes need it, my dear"—she smiled—"even from so wretched a man as you." And she watched me very steadily, with that steady smile.
> I said, after a moment, with difficulty, "True enough, dear lady. True enough. But I wonder why I feel so depressed."

IV

Tell Me How Long the Train's Been Gone ends with a doubled climax, by means of which the sexual and political themes come together. Barbara, the white lady love, is seduced by Christopher, the black boyfriend, while Leo Proudhammer is recovering from his heart attack. In itself, this fact is not especially shocking, human beings, white or black, being what they are; it is the utter cant, Baldwin's by now wearisome racial metaphysics, which the lady uses to explain the seduction, that *is* shocking:

> "I think *he* wanted"—she stopped—"I think *he* wanted to find out —if love was possible. If it was really possible. I think he had to find *out* what I thought of *his* body, by taking mine." She paused. "It wasn't like that," she said, "with you and me."

The political climax occurs a few pages later when Christopher explains to Proudhammer that "you got to agree that we need us some guns," and Proudhammer answers, "Yes, I see that." An uncharacteristic flash of intelligence overcomes him for a moment, however, and he says to Christopher, "But we're outnumbered you know." To which Christopher answers: "Shit. So were the early Christians."

Placed as it is at the end of the book, and as the last word spoken by any of the characters, Christopher's reply is clearly meant to be a decisive stroke, a sign of Baldwin's acquiescence. So let us look at it for a moment.

Some of the early Christians, presumably unlike the Black Nationalists of today, *wanted* to die, since they looked upon martyrdom as an avenue to paradise and did not care whether they were outnumbered or not. Hence, they can hardly be taken as a significant model for young blacks, unless Baldwin is proposing (what hardly seems likely) a parallel course of sanctification through suicide. Other early Christians—and by now, no longer so early—had as their goal not the destruction of the oppressive state, presumably the goal of the Black Nationalists today, but rather a gradual infiltration into places of power. This, indeed, is what happened: the Christians, slowly transforming the nature of their belief, took over the Empire, or if you wish, the Empire took over Christianity. So, again, Christopher's comparison has no relevance to the present moment. But finally there is the not inconsequential fact that the early Christians, who were absolute pacifists, never said, "we need us some guns," and never proposed to destroy the Roman state as a tiny minority shooting it out with an oppressive majority. Again, therefore, the proposal to employ guns cannot be rationalized as a tactic or justified as a morality by comparison with the "early Christians." What, then, is the force of Christopher's remark? Its force—and I believe that for many readers it will have a notable force—lies simply in the assumption that not many people will trouble to think about it critically and indeed that the current intellectual atmosphere in this country discourages people from thinking.

Tell Me How Long the Train's Been Gone will appeal to the liberal white devils who buy books and who now think, some of them, that it is fashionable to look with kindliness on the Black Panthers and to speak—after all, it's not *their* blood—with approval about the fantasies of apocalypse being nurtured in certain academic and black circles. As such, the novel is a document of and for the moment, an emblem of the 'sixties.

Strangely, however, it also shows, in a few scenes, what Baldwin's true gift as a novelist might be. It is not a gift for sexual *Sturm und Drang,* whether hetero or homo or bi; nor for militant protest; nor for political prophecy. Baldwin's true gift as a novelist is for comedy of manners, nuanced observation, refinement of detail. How absurd and painful that in *this* book Baldwin should now and again show a kinship with the kind of fine-threaded fiction written by . . . Jane Austen. There is, for instance, a fine scene in which the young actors at the summer theater meet some local Negroes, have an uncomfortable dinner with them, and go off warily to a black gin mill: it is all done with control and exactness. There is a nice bit in which Leo and his parents go out on the streets of Harlem to shop, and the playfulness of the older people breaks out for a minute. There is a good section in which Leo works in a restaurant owned by a tough Jamaican woman, and Baldwin can describe with neat detail their division of labor, responsibility, and emotion.

But this is not a moment in which our culture can encourage a writer to develop a small talent. This is a moment when writers feel driven to destroy themselves: with comforts of doom, illusions of prophecy, rhetoric of blood.

A Fiery Baptism

by Calvin C. Hernton

I

In "Blood of the Lamb," I made several analytical predictions.[1] One was that Baldwin's writing would undergo a fiery baptism; I also asserted that when this happened the vicarious and pornographic romance that white Americans were carrying on with him would quietly cease.

The truth of this assertion was confirmed when James Baldwin wrote his play, *Blues for Mister Charlie,* and by the manner in which the white world reacted to its production. The play was brute, crude, violent, and bold, more in the fashion of Richard Wright (or LeRoi Jones whom I will come to later) than of the usual suffering, pleading, metaphysical Baldwin of *The Fire Next Time* and prior works.

Unlike most plays written by Negroes, *Blues for Mister Charlie* is not about civil rights or any of the other "acceptable" subjects on Negro-white relations. The play is based on the Emmett Till murder case of 1955, and it deals with the sexual variable, which is perhaps the most hushed-up and yet the most explosive factor involved in racism in the United States. And Baldwin's treatment of it is so straightforward, realistic and secular that whites found it difficult to face what they have been hiding and gliding over for centuries. Moreover, this Baldwin—the *Blues for Mister Charlie* Baldwin—is an aggressive, a masculine Baldwin. Add to this the fact that the sexuality of the Negroes in the play is earthy, rich, full of power and human animalism—all of which Baldwin does not

[1] Sections I and II of this postscript were written during the latter part of 1965 in New York, one year after I wrote "Blood of the Lamb." Four years later, in 1969, I revised and augmented this postscript in London. I have dated the sections.

apologize for, but affirms with dignity and prowess. It was simply too much for the majority of whites to accept or seriously consider.

For instance, both times I saw the play there were as many, if not more, whites in the audience than there were Negroes. One could not help but feel the negative vibrations radiating from the whites during the major portion of the evening. They seemed to squirm throughout the play and grow little in their seats; many tried to hold a straight face (face of chalk), but one could see and feel the hot charge boiling beneath their white masks. Upon two occasions— (a) when Richard (the Negro hero), back down South telling his friends how many white girls he has slept with up North, is showing a photograph of a girl with long hair and remarks, "Man, you know where all that hair's been"; and (b) when Richard tells Lyle, (the Southern bigot) who has been threatening him, "Man, are you scared I'm going to get in your wife's drawers?"—I thought half of the white audience might jump up and storm out of the theater. But they held onto their seats. Again, after Richard has been murdered by Lyle, and Juanita (Richard's sweetheart, played by Diana Sands) in lamentation delivers her speech on how Richard made love to her, desciibing it in plain but powerful language, telling how she took Richard into her womb and how she "grind" him and how meaningful the act was—again, I saw the theater faces of white people twist and contort in agony and revulsion. In fact, the white ladies sitting next to me began gossiping very rapidly about the careers of Rip Torn (Lyle) and Pat Hingle (Parnell, the Southern liberal) as if nothing was happening on stage at all. And the applause of the whites—one got the impression that it was as much out of nervous reaction to cover up embarrassment as it was an expression of honest enthusiasm.

On the other hand, Negroes seemed to be enthralled with delight and moral vindication to see for the first time the true nature of their lives, and their plight, played back to them with dignity and no beating around the bush. Many Negroes were there with white companions. I recall one tall dark Negro who is a famous man. He came in with his white girl and sat down as if he was out for the usual "highbrow" theater evening. Before the play was half through, the Negro had unbuttoned his collar, had reared back in his seat, and was looking around as if he himself had written *Blues for Mister Charlie*. Pride was bursting on his face and chest.

Not only did whites in general recoil from the play, but the press, in most cases, reviewed something other than what the play was. The majority of reviewers said the play failed as a "civil rights" play. Those few who admitted what the play was about found ways of debunking it as far-fetched, saying that Richard got lynched because he "asked for it" (*The Village Voice*, April 30, 1964). Only one reviewer wrote a favorable piece about the play. His name is Tom Driver and he has since resigned mysteriously from *The Reporter*. His favorable review was not printed in the magazine.

What Tom Driver said in his review (which was eventually published in the *Negro Digest, The Village Voice,* and *Christianity and Crisis*) was that the *virtues* of the play killed it. He praised the language of the play, which was raw, earthy, and full of four-letter words (and caused whites to shiver in their seats). After lauding Diana Sands' portrayal as the "best performance any American actress has given this year," Driver went on to affirm the essential reality of the play: that the white man (and woman) in America has a sexual hang-up about himself vis-à-vis the Negro, and it is this hang-up that terrifies the white man whenever he encounters the Negro, and that causes so much violence and bloodshed. Most of all, Driver viewed favorably Baldwin's stereotyped projection of Southern Negroes and whites; that is, the "sterile and sexually insecure" white male who places his "lily-white" wife upon a pedestal while he slips around at night with Negro women, and the "virile and lusty" Negro who enjoys the sex act to the fullest without guilt or reservations. Parnell, the Southern liberal, confesses his deep sexual involvement with a Negro woman. Lyle, the Southern bigot who is so afraid that Richard is after his wife, brags about how he has taken the bodies of many Negro girls. In fact, Lyle is really interested in Richard's sweetheart Juanita, rather than the other way around. And Jo (Lyle's wife, brilliantly played by Ann Wedgeworth), the typical fragile and neglected Southern "lady" who usually knows about her husband's clandestine behavior with black women and who herself has come to accept all the stereotyped notions and emotions about and toward the Negro, leaps (almost gladly!) to comply with her husband's accusation that Richard has "attacked" her when the latter came to Lyle's store to buy a Coke. In reality Richard never touched the woman and she knows it; yet in court she testifies to the contrary, and Lyle is set free *for* murdering Richard. After which Lyle brags again, "Hell yes, I killed that nigger," and is glad of it.

We "liberals" in America always want justice to win out in the end. Well, in the South there is no justice when it comes to the Negro. And Baldwin wrote it as it really is. The murderers of countless Emmett Tills are still running amuck throughout the entire South.

As I have indicated, many of the reviewers accused Baldwin of not writing a play, "technically" speaking. Well now, several of the plays of Arthur Miller, Eugene O'Neill, Clifford Odets, and others (*The Deputy*, by Rolf Hochhuth, for instance) are not plays, "technically" speaking. Yet such plays enjoy successful runs on as well as off Broadway. Any art form, I say art *form*, that deals with man's inhumanity to man and does not end with "justice winning out" or "crime does not pay" is viewed and reviewed in America as "controversial." Let's come closer to home. In regard to the Negro, when the white man is portrayed as a barbarous, unmitigated bigot, we not only label the art form as "controversial," we also cry out that it is not "art"; we call it "propaganda." Specifically, *Blues for Mister Charlie* hits white America between the eyes, and does not apologize for doing so. Evidently to talk about the white man's sexual fears and guilts is to strike him in the most vulnerable corners of his ego. And he loses all rationality, all objectivity. He either goes blank or he tries to absolve his guilt by simpleminded rationalizations. For instance, Michael Smith (*The Village Voice*, April 30, 1964) claims, ". . . Lyle kills Richard not so much because he is a Negro as because he asks for it." Later Smith asserts, "Lyle, more in defense of his sex-self-respect than of his race, murders Richard."

Unfortunately (or is it fortunately?) these remarks reveal more about Mr. Smith than they do about *Blues for Mister Charlie*. First of all, Richard does not behave around whites (Lyle and his wife) according to the "bowing-and-scraping" pattern that bigoted whites demand in the South. No, Richard walks and talks like a man who is aware of his dignity and inherent equality as a human being. To the psychotic white in the South this takes on a sexual meaning; it is perceived as sexual assault. Secondly, the only sexual self-respect Lyle has is a false one, a guilty one shot through with and based on white male supremacy! Doesn't Mr. Smith know that sexual guilt and paranoia are intricate aspects of racism in America? James Baldwin does! And thirdly, if Richard is "mean and tormented and looking for trouble," why is he mean, by what is he tormented? But most of all, Mr. Smith, like his Southern counterpart, seems to interpret Richard's "talking back" and standing up to Lyle and his wife as "looking for trouble."

I suppose that great numbers of Negroes in the South today are standing up and talking back and demanding human respect and in the process are "looking for trouble." I suppose that their endeavoring to secure their God-given rights and make America a better place in which ALL Americans can live means, with reference to their lynching, that Medgar Evers and James Chaney and countless others "asked for it." And finally, while throughout the decades the sexuality as well as the general behavior traits of Negroes has been thought of and portrayed as vulgar, subhuman and derogative, it is a telling thing that only when these same traits are portrayed with prowess and dignity against the barbarity, both sexual and otherwise, of whites, that only then (only now!) white men rise up to shout down intrusions. My grandmother used to say, "The ones who yell the loudest is the culprits with the mostest to hide."

In fact, there seemed to have been, at one time or another, an inside move to kill *Blues for Mister Charlie* before it came to its natural end, if indeed its end was natural. One day, an editor of a New York magazine called the box office for ticket reservations and was told by someone that all seats were sold out. The same editor waited several hours and called again, for he had been told such would happen and, behold, he was informed this time by another person that there were plenty of tickets available. I also understand that someone significantly connected with the play was quoted as having said, "Before I will have the things said about white men that are being said upon that stage, I'd as soon go broke."

Now, what does all this mean in terms of Baldwin's development as a writer and as a Negro? First, as a writer he is no longer addressing a predominantly white audience, at least no longer in the guilt-soothing terms that characterized most of his previous essays. In *Blues for Mister Charlie* he was no longer dealing exclusively with the subjective or moral coefficients of the white world's inhumanity toward the Negro. Rather, Baldwin was dealing with the raw, brute, objective facts of the white man's barbarity toward black people in America. Along with the terrible facts, there are the white man's fears, anxieties, and most of all, his guilt! *Blues for Mister Charlie* plowed deep into the very psyche of white America; with justified animosity and vindictiveness it hurled all of his atrocious deeds and horrible guilts solidly back into the white man's face! And seemingly it was too much for whites to bear. But Negroes loved it.

Which means that Baldwin, as a Negro, is writing less to soothe white folks' guilt and more to enlighten, dignify and anger American Negroes. With *Blues for Mister Charlie,* Baldwin plunged into the position of being a true spokesman not just for the middle class but for the masses of his people. Michael Smith of *The Village Voice* made this observation and added that it was "unfortunate," claiming that being a spokesman for the Negro nearly prevented Baldwin from being an "artist." Why is it that after the production of *Blues for Mister Charlie* appeared the very same whites who used to praise Baldwin now rise up to put him down!

Baldwin is not merely a writer. He is a Negro writer, and we Americans—especially white Americans—have seen to that and no doubt will continue to see to it for a long time hence. The question of whether *Blues for Mister Charlie* was artistically a bad play is about as relevant to the real issue as saying that *Crime and Punishment* is artistically a bulky, sloppy novel, which it certainly is. To wit, *Another Country* is so bad artistically that I am relatively sure its publication had little to do with art. But the critics "raved." They did not talk about the artistry of the book, but about how "bold" it was. With drooling mouths the public consumed it to the ticker tape of the best-seller lists. I saw them on subways, on buses, at lunch counters and midtown Madison Avenue restaurants—especially the young, up-and-coming, clean-shaven, no-mustached, gray-flanneled. Coming and going, I saw them reading about the country of A-not-her! Talk about art vs. propaganda. *Another Country* was almost nothing but propaganda; propaganda for homosexuality. I am definitely not making a moral judgment about homosexuality as artistic subject matter, or about James Baldwin. I *am* making a moral analysis of the character of white Americans in regard to their good faith when it comes to facing up to the social, political, economic and sexual horrors, in artistic presentations as well as in reality, that have been and are being heaped upon the American Negro. It seems—and this is the real issue—that whites in *this* country, despite an abundance of liberalism, are not yet morally capable of accepting any open presentation, on the one hand, of their sexual feelings regarding black men, and on the other hand, of the sexual depravity that white men (especially Southerners) have historically inflicted upon Negro women, the guilt stemming from it. This is what killed *Blues for Mister Charlie* and, in my opinion, severed the romantic involvement between James Baldwin and white America, forever.

Although James Baldwin may not sell as many books and will not be so affectionately discussed in white circles, or for that matter in lily-nice, middle-class Negro circles, the cessation of the romance represents a step forward rather than a stumble backward. Characteristically, Baldwin has written of the race problem, or of Negro-white relations, with a deep burning love (submission) that was rooted in the religion of the long-suffering. Repeatedly, incessantly, James Baldwin has pleaded with passion for forgiveness and love between whites and blacks as the solution for the nightmare that makes havoc of our lives. But, I believe, it has become apparent to Baldwin that the probability of a cleansing love and forgiveness between Negroes and whites is long in forthcoming. America is one of the most spiritually bankrupt countries in a world where it is, as Baldwin must know by now, terribly difficult to create and maintain a personal love, let alone love of mankind. But this is not to say that we will no longer see in Baldwin's work the influence of a deeply religious man. Emile Capouya, a former editor at Macmillan who once shared an apartment with Baldwin, pointed out in 1963 in a lecture at the New School for Social Research that James Baldwin is not really a deep thinker in the sense of an academic or even a rugged intellectual; rather, he is a provincial preacher with a grand intelligence for literary style and eloquence—and he is at his best, as can be seen by comparing his essays with his fiction, when he is writing out of the depths of his spiritual background. And this background will continue to echo in his labor—no matter how charged otherwise with secular rage—until he lays his pen down and saunters into elemental peace.

II

One final contention must be resolved. While James Baldwin was being called, with reference to the race problem, the "conscience of the nation," I wrote that as a writer he stood at the head of a group of emerging black artists and writers, in particular those whom I called the Existential Negroes. First of all, Baldwin's existentialism is rooted in religion, in spirituality, in the metaphysical. This means that (a) in analyzing the race problem Baldwin has dwelt primarily with aspects such as *hate, anguish, guilt, conscience, internal torture, sin* and *iniquity*—his favorite term, I believe, is a word which applies a "riddle" or a "mystery" to race relations: *conundrum;* (b) when it comes to alleviating the race problem his key concepts include *love, redemption, cleansing the heart, forgiveness, endurance* and so on. If the elements of a situation are viewed in religious terms, then it follows that the resolution of the situation must come in and through religious measures such as, for instance, forgiveness.

Specifically, James Baldwin is a *religious* existentialist. His task, whether he intended it or not, has been, as it were, to clear the air of all moral or metaphysical issues and cobwebs, and to define, in the realm of spirituality, what must be done to end the nightmare of our lives. Notice, he always speaks in terms of "our"—which is to say both white and Negro.

Baldwin has performed (and only God knows how!) his task excellently. He has made our hearts tremble, his words have filled us with compassion, and the genius of his consternation has enthralled and whiplashed our consciences. In a word, James *The Fire Next Time* Baldwin has caused us to weep. But beyond this nothing more has ensued. And that is as it should be, for as we all know Americans have a peculiar kind of religion whereby we go to church on Sunday and weep and confess our guilts, only to go the rest of the week and commit the same crimes. But do not play Baldwin cheap. He has, perhaps inadvertently, proved his point masterfully—no amount of mere preaching is going to cause white people to go out in the real world and undo the objective socio-political and economic conditions which they have instituted in order to prevent the Negro from realizing the fruits of American democracy. And the awareness of this has inspired, has necessitated, on the part of other Negro writers, the assumption of a secular rather than religious frame of reference when handling subject matter that deals with the race problem. These writers—no matter what they say—owe James Baldwin, as he owes Richard Wright, a great deal. Before we get to them though, let us consider Baldwin's latest major work and see what observations can be made in the light of everything I have said about the man and his writing so far.

III

London, 1969

The big four-hundred-page novel *Tell Me How Long the Train's Been Gone* (published in 1968) left me rather disappointed. Baldwin, as I have stated, is one of the best essayists in the world. He is also a novelist who toils like a ditchdigger. *Tell Me How Long* is full of labor and it works, although I personally find it void of the stuff that grips me in the gut and makes me want to move. But this is Baldwin's business. Any writer worth his typewriter will write what he alone chooses and not what somebody tries to dictate to him, and that's cool by me. I, moreover, do not demand that an artist top himself every time. A writer may write about the same things involving the same elements for as long as he lives. Edna O'Brien, Erskine Caldwell, Mickey Spillane, Frank Yerby, Pearl Buck, to name a few, are classic examples. But each time there should be a new dimension, a new depth, a new *something;* the same people and the same general problems, all right, but the nature of the specific problem must somehow emerge as a qualitatively new or different story. No matter how skillfully rendered or disguised, rehashing the same joke or the same sob story becomes a drag for a lot of people after a while. Unless the writer and the people are hooked on the vicarious enema of the soap opera.

Richard Wright is dead now. Baldwin's father, I assume, has long been dead. Yet once again the dead is resurrected—he is the same father, the same decrepit nigger that has appeared in almost everything Baldwin has written. Only now the father is *multiplied* (more fathers to kill?). After the real father is denigrated to death, lo and behold up jumps the hero's older brother, Caleb, who turns out to be not much more than a metamorphosized version of the same Harlem pork-chop nigger preacher that the original father was. Before this happens though, the hero (whose name is Leo) and his brother are not only wedded together by virtue of their common front against the father and against the terror-laden streets of Harlem, but they are seen as boyhood lovers. Leo loves his brother with such compassion that he comforts him by making love to him one night as they lie together in their bed. Later—on the battlefield of war—the brother undergoes a conversion experience and comes away from the war a transformed man.

Leo (his last name is Proudhammer) is struggling to become an actor. His brother, who has now become God's humble black representative, frowns on the life Leo is leading (with those immoral actor types) and cannot see any future in Leo's pursuing such an ungodly and unheard of profession—unheard of, especially where a Negro is concerned. Caleb castigates Leo for not getting a "real" job and settling down to lead a decent God-fearing life among his own people. The gulf between the two brothers, the late-boyhood lovers, is widened and can never be bridged. Leo hates God and curses Him not only for what He has done to his brother, who now is a replica of their despicable father; but also for the role that God, or religion, has historically played in molding all but a few black people into obsequious Bible-jibbering nonentities (Uncle Toms) in the unmitigated grip of oppression and terror. The relationship, however, is maintained symbiotically, but with hidden resentment on both sides, mainly out of reverence for the tenderness of their childhood love, and more significantly because Leo does actually become a superstar on the stage—"nothing succeeds like success!"

It seems to me that what I have termed the "pater-fallacy" in Baldwin's writing (if not in his actual life) is much more than a mere hang-up, for now the obsession with the father comes across as nothing less than Patricidal Mania. The hopelessly eternal recurrence (as in Freudian mythology, or as in the Bible) of the son's scheming and struggling to take the father's place by first having him and then destroying him. But with Baldwin it is repeated over and over again. How long must the characters in his works go on blaming and hating and loving and killing the *same* father?

Moreover there is the exact repetition of certain other motifs: (1) incest homosexuality; both in the restricted and the broader sense, the hero usually has a love-hate relationship with the father. But now this relationship occurs with the brother also, and eventually the hero goes on to have it with everybody, especially men; (2) the hero is inevitably narcissistic—he worships himself, his body, his desires, his ambitions, his sensitivities, his pains, his joys with an all-consuming passion; (3) although the hero might screw a few women, such occasions are never as meaningful or as powerfully felt as the relationships he has with men; (4) the hero is self-riddled —while he loves himself, he also loathes himself; while he loves his race, he also feels disgust toward it; while he hates white people, he also is haunted by love for them; (5) the hero is always alarmingly honest, thus he is virtuous; and (6) everything always harks back to the same set of background circumstances. The repetition of these things in *Tell Me How Long the Train's Been Gone* makes the book resemble too closely nothing but a reshuffling of the same old cards in the same old games.

I do not take back what I said about Baldwin's having become a great writer—I've said it enough. But no matter how great he is, he does not seem to have anything new or different or progressive to say anymore. This could very well mean that, among other things, Baldwin has unwittingly or wittingly written himself into the very species personage that he has seemingly been trying to destroy, the species personage of The Father. Whether this is true or not, or whether it is true for a certain period, it is clear that he has necessitated if not nurtured into being a radically different set of black writers from himself and, alas, has been eclipsed by them.

Let me make one thing absolutely clear. These writers are not in competition with James Baldwin, nor are they in conflict with him. Nor can anyone take Baldwin's "place" as a writer, and certainly not as a black writer. Baldwin is an individual writer in his own right. (All writers are individual writers in their own right.) The sooner this is recognized the sooner black writers will stop falling for the white man's trick of "Who's Going To Be Our Next Great Token Nigger Writer While the Rest of You Fight Among Yourselves!"

Certain writers may be distinguished from each other according to how much they differ in terms of style, subject matter, point of view, and so on. What I am saying here is that a revolutionary new genre of black writing has arrived on the scene. The new artists are doing their thing, which extends beyond and is categorically distinguishable from the characteristic manner in which Baldwin has been doing his thing. The results, in terms of response and effect, are and will continue to be markedly different from the way whites and blacks have been affected by, or have responded to, James Baldwin.

Fathers and Sons in James Baldwin's
Go Tell It on the Mountain

by Michel Fabre

Go Tell It on the Mountain treats the conversion of a black adolescent who, on his fourteenth birthday, adopts his family's religion in a Harlem storefront church. The protagonist, Johnny Grimes, laying increasing claim to our attention, proposes himself as the sole hero. On looking closer, however, the reader discovers that fewer than half of the three hundred odd pages of the novel express John's point of view, and these are found at the beginning and end of the tale, like the side panels of a triptych whose central panel ("The Prayers of the Saints") relates the converging stories of Johnny's aunt, stepfather, and mother. These characters lean on their past in such a way that the figure of Gabriel, with the stories of Florence and Elizabeth on either side, emerges a little like Christ between the Holy Women. In this "retable novel," Johnny indeed reappears in each section, but a bit like the donor depicted on a small scale in each panel of the painting. Gabriel usurps first place. The son is dispossessed of his story by the fate of his father. The father stays in the foreground as long as the two women combined, and his presence casts a threatening shadow over the space in the novel reserved for Johnny. As early as the second line, the child's future is defined by his relationship to his father: "Everyone has always said that John would be a preacher when he grew up, just like his father."

Like a folktale, from which there are archetypal resonances now and then, this story seems to have no other function than the fulfillment of this prophecy. It ends with a final confrontation:

"Pères et fils dans *Go Tell It on the Mountain*, de James Baldwin" by Michel Fabre. From *Études Anglaises*, 23, no. 1 (1970), 47–61. Translated by Keneth Kinnamon. Used by permission of Michel Fabre.

> He turned to face his father—he found himself smiling, but his father did not smile.
>
> They looked at each other a moment. His mother stood in the doorway, in the long shadows of the hall. (303) [1]

As is right, the mother stays in the shadow, withdrawn.

Linguistic recurrences corroborate this structural arrangement of the novel. In John's story, words designating the father are twice as numerous as those designating the mother (three times as numerous in the last section, which relates the spiritual confrontation between father and son). In "Gabriel's Prayer," expressions applying to the Lord predominate, as they should in the mouth of a preacher (at a rate of more than two per page), but the son takes second place. The pastor defines himself less as a consequence of his three successive women than in terms of the line of saints that he must beget in order to know that he is set down in the Divine Plan. And at the geometric center of the book is placed the crucial sentence summing up Gabriel's dilemma:

> It came to him that this living son, this headlong, living Royal, might be cursed for the sin of his mother, whose sin had never been truly repented; for that the living proof of her sin, he who knelt tonight, a very interloper among the saints, stood between her soul and God.

The interloper—in this case Johnny—not only comes between God and the salvation of her whose illegitimate son he is, but also between God and the salvation of his stepfather:

> How could there not be a difference between the son of a weak, proud woman and some careless boy, and the son that God had promised him, who would carry down the joyful line his father's name, and who would work until the day of the second coming to bring about His Father's Kingdom? (151)

Such is the question which the novel continually strives to answer. With Gabriel, the desire to see the prodigal son return doubles the fear of seeing "the son of the bondwoman" take his place. For the relationship of paternity gears itself down. It shatters like a mirror whose fragments reflect all possible combinations, fragments whose deceitful symmetry moves the plot along. The family

---

[1] All page numbers [which are enclosed in parentheses] refer to the Universal Library edition (New York: Grosset & Dunlap, 1961).

situation takes on an unsuspected complexity in its almost Faulk-
nerian unraveling: in Johnny's narrative, nothing apprises us that
Gabriel is not his father or justifies Gabriel's scornful harshness
toward the child. The explanation that presents itself at first is that
of an irrational preference for Roy, the younger of the boys. A
question of precedence would seem to be at stake, with John feeling himself dispossessed of his birthright. The mother loves both
sons equally. She favors Johnny for the time being (she is the only
one who does not forget his birthday) in order to compensate for
Gabriel's injustice, but she quickly comes back to Roy when he is
hurt. John examines himself in vain for the unaccountable blem-
ish that could be the cause of his rejection. He finds part of the
explanation in his own shortcomings: his Oedipus complex, his
desire to leave the ghetto, the intelligence which singles him out,
his resentment toward his father. This psychological explanation
gives way to a historical explanation only in "Gabriel's Prayer."
There is a double secret: Roy is indeed the son of Gabriel and
Elizabeth, but Johnny is the illegitimate son of Elizabeth and Richard, who died before he could marry her. John does not know this
and Gabriel cannot forget it. Moreover, the correspondence of bastardy is symmetrical: at the time of his first marriage to the sterile
Deborah, Gabriel himself had by Esther a bastard son, Royal. Royal
has been killed in a brawl, and Roy is a more legitimate substitute
in his father's heart. Their names—chosen by Gabriel to indicate
the line of kings he wants to beget—bring them together less than
their aggressive and rebellious temperaments inherited from their
father, and less still than their violent fates: the knife that cut the
throat of Royal has just disfigured Roy.

Elizabeth as well as Johnny is unaware of Gabriel's slip, and
Gabriel, like a Pharisee, can consider her as a former sinner whose
illegitimate fruit he stigmatizes because his own sin of a similar
nature remains unsuspected. Only Florence, the pastor's sister,
could reveal his offense, of which she has irrefutable proof in the
form of a compromising letter. Accordingly she appears as Johnny's
fairy godmother: she has already protected him, just as Elizabeth
has, from Gabriel's blazing wrath, and the weapon she holds could
make Gabriel vulnerable. Here the plot seems to join again the
archetypal situation of the folktale: a stranger is about to dethrone
a tyrant with the aid of a woman who gives him a talisman and
also, as we shall see, with the effectual support of a companion of

his own age. But this situation is not exploited because Baldwin himself prefers a symbolic form more appropriate to the religious context of the novel, that of an Old Testament struggle for succession.

Moreover, this relationship is complicated by the inability of fathers and sons (like husbands and wives) to come together. Mutual love is forbidden, it seems, as much by virtue of a psychological fatality, holiness as opposed to happiness, as by a divine order, the saint being in reality a damned soul. In order to mortify his flesh, Gabriel marries Deborah, who has been stripped of her graceful and fecund femininity by being raped by some white men. This woman, who loves him and whom he does not love, cannot give him a legitimate heir. Esther, the woman whom he desires and who loves him completely, bears him a son when he does not want to marry her. From this situation proceeds a drama of impossible recognition: Gabriel cannot legitimize the child that he loves tenderly, and the child cannot know who his father is. Irony of fate or immanent justice: Royal, when the pastor walks by, makes a classic and coarse joke about his sexual potency without knowing that he himself is the living proof of that potency. And the only moment when Gabriel can call (metaphorically) Royal his son is the moment when the danger of being castrated by whites brings them together.

After the deaths of Royal and Deborah, Gabriel accepts as a sign of the Lord the meeting—brought about by Florence—with Elizabeth and her son. They are sent to him, he thinks, so that he can expiate his own sin by marrying a repentant sinner. The drama might then have resolved itself, but the pastor's egoism and bad faith had prevented him from bringing up Johnny as his own son. The child represents Elizabeth's sin to Gabriel's eyes, but also a means of projecting and of rejecting his own guilt. Ready to love, Johnny encounters a hatred which compels him to hate in order to survive. He becomes the anti-son ("the Devil's son"), and Gabriel turns into the anti-father. Roy's birth finally brings a legitimate offspring to the pastor, but Roy rejects his heritage. The real son calls his father "bastard," a term that Gabriel hypocritically feels loathe to hear Esther apply to Royal, but that he himself readily applies to Johnny. And as Roy, the prodigal son, leaves the fold, the adopted son tries to enter it and succeeds only to the extent that he is a prodigal son.

Moreover, just as Esther's existence is shadowy for Elizabeth,

Richard's existence is obscure to Gabriel. And for Johnny, his actual father Richard does not exist at all. He is defined for the reader only as the mythic father adorned with all the qualities which contrast with Gabriel: he was handsome, intelligent, generous, life-loving, desirous of learning and improving himself. Some of these qualities are Johnny's inheritance, just as perhaps that weakness of character, connected to his feeling of dignity, which led Richard to slash his wrists after being put in jail.

Thus the novel plays with a constellation of fathers—unknown and mythical father, real and legitimate father, putative father, possible father, adulterous husband and father of a bastard. This corresponds to a whole constellation of sons—natural, adulterine, adoptive, prodigal, etc. These are merely the different roles assumed by Richard, Gabriel, Johnny, Roy, and Royal in a tragic game of hide-and-seek. The novel derives its plot from this tragicomedy of errors. If the author were sticking to the *deus ex machina* of classical drama, it would suffice to unveil the mistake in order to resolve the enigma. Curiously, however, only the reader is aware of everything in *Go Tell It on the Mountain*. Johnny learns nothing: the existence of his real father remains as hidden from him as that of Gabriel's bastard. In a last gesture of cruelty toward the brother that she has always hated because he had taken away first place in their mother's heart, Florence threatens to reveal everything: "It'll make Elizabeth to know," she said, "that she ain't the only sinner . . . in your holy house. And little Johnny, there—he'll know he ain't the only bastard." (293)

Johnny's discovery that he is a bastard would be in effect a glorious revelation because the shame of his illegitimacy would be put in the shade by the glory of having as perfect a being as Richard for his father, and his shame would be annulled by the discovery of the first Royal's existence. But Florence does not speak. This logical and "mechanical" resolution could only take place with authority in a problematic "fifth act."

If mutual recognition and reconciliation are not the result of an artificial intervention by Florence, it would seem to be because Baldwin wishes to bring them about by divine intervention. In effect, at the moment of his conversion, when the saints are praying before the tabernacle, Johnny becomes conscious of his identity and his heritage, and they take root in the discovery and acceptance of his own sin. Religion appears as a mode of knowing a self guilty of transgressions against purity, charity, and racial and human solidarity.

John would like to escape the prophecy: "He would not be like his father, or his father's fathers. He would have another life." (15) An ambiguous and multiple denial. He refuses either to be a preacher or to become a "leader of his race." At one moment he chooses material success—to be well fed, to dress well, to go to the movies—what is equivalent to rejecting his racial as well as his religious heritage. The trip to downtown Manhattan presents this symbolic meaning: from the top of the hill in Central Park, Johnny dominates the city as Rastignac did Paris. But by attending the movies he carries out not an act of social participation but a gesture of defiance with regard both to morality and to religion, because he identifies with the white heroine, a rebel who "tells the world to kiss her ass."

In his intelligence Johnny has discovered an almost magical power, a way to salvation that the others do not have. What does he hope to get from it? Only love: "Perhaps, with this power he might one day win that love which he so longed for." (17) But inner force and power to make oneself loved are inseparable from the capacity to resist and to hate. The boy cherishes and preserves both, unable to prevent their being connected to the evil force that his father wants to whip out of him. He admits that he is searching for hate as much as for love. He lives for the day when he can curse his father on his deathbed. His individual survival necessitates this hatred, and the hatred prevents him from being truly converted, for a hierarchical reason:

> His father was God's minister, the ambassador of the King of Heaven, and John could not bow before the throne of grace without first kneeling to his father. On his refusal to do this had his life depended, and John's secret heart had flourished in its wickedness until the day his sin first overtook him. (17–18)

His sacred function protects his father, who does not abstain from using religion as an instrument of his power. Religion prohibits the son from being himself unless he finds a way to annul the prohibition or make a shield of it. But, Baldwin says, Johnny's sin catches him up. This sin is the discovery of his sexuality, which

is felt by him as an abyss. Woman is present everywhere: Ella Mae
at the church service, with her her breasts and thighs under her thin
robes, at the side of the handsome youth Elisha; the stain on the
ceiling that takes on female form; the couple that John sees making
love standing up against a wall; the temptations of the street . . .
[Fabre's punctuation]. Woman is also, first of all, his mother. When
Johnny, cleaning the kitchen, muses: "He who is filthy, let him be
filthy still," he looks immediately at his mother and sees her face
as in her youthful photograph, the face of a desirable woman ready
to be taken. The Oedipus complex is everywhere. The son is sexually jealous of his father and of that virility which fills him with
disgust. In the bathroom (the place of sin, which connects his solitary sin and his voyeurism) he, like Noah's son, has looked at "his
father's hideous nakedness. It was secret, like sin, and slimy,
like the serpent, and heavy, like the rod. Then he hated his father,
and longed for the power to cut his father down." (267) The allusion is clear: castrate the father, possess the rod—sex and scepter.
And the symbolic serpent is found again, in bronze, poised to strike,
among the very important family photographs. The voyeurism that
makes John "diabolical" is his revenge, for it reveals his father's
transgression:

> "I know what you do in the dark, black man, when you think the
> Devil's son's asleep. I heard you, spitting, and groaning, and chok-
> ing—and I *seen* you, riding up and down, and going in and out.
> . . . I don't care about your long white robe. I seen you under the
> robe, I seen you!" (269)

Through the paternal puritanism, very normal instincts appear
to John to be the proof of his damnation. Swamped by his guilt,
he dreams of his punishment. It is the terror of castration: "His
father raised his hand. The knife came down." (270) Thus the knife
joins Gabriel's three sons together as possible victims in a parody
of Abraham's sacrifice. But Johnny is dreaming. He is not a true
son, and the knife will not score him. In his mystical trance at the
foot of the altar, he projects his phantasms and assumes his sin.
Such is the role of religion: to help man to objectify his terrors and
set them aside. And religion furnishes the adolescent a means of
disqualifying his father before dominating him: he becomes the
son of God in order to count Him an ally. This implies, literally, a
rebirth, a second coming into the world:

Sown in dishonor, he would be raised in honor: he would have been born again.[2]

Then he would no longer be the son of his father, but the son of his Heavenly Father, the King. Then he need no longer fear his father, for he could take, as it were, their quarrel over his father's head to Heaven—to the Father who loved him. . . . Then he and his father would be equals. . . . His father could not cast him out, whom God had gathered in. (194)

Accordingly, John puts God in his service, apparently to rejoin his father in a shared affection, but in reality to supersede him. He dreams of hating until the end of time this "eternal father" who must die so that he will no longer block his path. Having become the Lord's anointed, he can vanquish Gabriel on the same ground where Gabriel has formerly supplanted the fathers of the church: by becoming a better preacher, John will be a saint, one of the elect, inviolable.

Furthermore, John mobilizes an "accomplice in salvation" in order to speak to God through this intermediary without respecting the hierarchy in which his father figures among his immediate superiors. This is Elisha, the prophet, the big brother, the young priest, but also the ephebe, the excessively beautiful guardian angel. When Gabriel lifts his hand to punish the adolescent whose impudent look pries into the depths of his soul, Elisha is both literally and physically interposed between John and his father. Elisha represents to John the ideal being, handsome, robust, angelic. Like Jacob with the angel, John has wrestled with Elisha in the empty chapel, and he has almost equaled his strength in an embrace in which tenderness mingles with homosexuality. A character such as Elisha is in effect as ambiguous as love between men, and under diverse appearances he recurs in all of Baldwin's works. In "The Outing," he is a substitute for the father: it is to David his big brother that Johnny devotes himself after his father has humiliated him in public, and the scene is haloed with a copper-colored sun, golden joy, and a quasi-divine presence. In *Go Tell It on the Mountain*, Elisha stands by John in his ecstasy; like Jesus, he orders, "Arise and walk!"; like the Creator in the frescoes of the Sistine Chapel, he stretches his hand to man:

[2] The references to dishonor and to John's illegitimacy are numerous, even in his part of the narration, but always in ambiguous terms. If he did know, his anguish would disappear, because he could hate his stepfather and dream of his true father.

"Rise up, Johnny," said Elisha, again. "Are you saved, boy?" . . .
Elisha stretched out his hand, and John took the hand, and stood
—so suddenly, and so strangely, and with such wonder!—once more
on his feet. (280)

Elisha bears witness to John's salvation and invulnerability. He
sponsors his rebirth in a scene that could not be more symbolic:

"He come through," cried Elisha, "didn't he, Deacon Grimes? The
Lord done laid him out, and turned him around and wrote his *new*
name down in glory. Bless our God!"
And he kissed John on the forehead, a holy kiss. . . . The sun
. . . fell over Elisha like a golden robe, and struck John's forehead,
where Elisha had kissed him, like a seal ineffaceable forever. (302)

Invited by Elisha to acknowledge that henceforth Johnny is
among the elect, Gabriel refuses. He does not reply, he does not
smile at Johnny, he gives no sign of admitting his defeat. Equality
among the saints does not imply their mutual acknowledgment,
and Johnny feels superior because he has already, in his power,
superseded the deacon in his ecclesiastical functions. Exploiting
the expedient of religion to affirm his identity as the old man had
used it to deny his sin, the young preacher brings about a murder
of his father quite as effectual as it is symbolic. The church is a
holy place where the adolescent escapes from the world, but also
the tabernacle where he escapes from his father and the place of
combat, the ring, where he triumphs over him.[3] As Johnny's intense resentment allows him to anticipate, his rediscovery of Gabriel is fake, and no relation of equality is established between
them. The conversion is carried out for other ends than the Lord's
service; it becomes a trick to escape the ghetto and his father, what
Baldwin calls "a gimmick" in *The Fire Next Time.* Therefore it
is normal that the liberation is illusory. A more effectual illusion
than the others is added to Johnny's childish dreams, those dreams
of grandeur in which he ceases to be the ugly duckling. Like the
author, we sympathize with the protagonist, but we suffer to see
verified his inability to liberate himself. His identity remains that
of a child. God the Almighty Father does not permit a sentimental

[3] There is in the novel an entire symbolism of space: Broadway and the strait
gate of ecstasy; the threshing-floor, the space marked off for separating the grain
from the chaff; the fall into the abyss and the flight on eagle's wings. The closed
square, ring, pulpit, threshing-floor are *par excellence* the place of trial and
triumph. Similarly, in "Sonny's Blues" the scene of the night club represents
the holy tabernacle.

reconciliation with his father, and both the psychological and the dramatic design carry over the denouement into a "fifth act."

One of the reasons that a denouement is impossible is found, perhaps, in the multiplicity of metaphorical functions that the author imposes on John's story. His destiny is presented as a quest for identity and the entire episode as an initiation. The story re-enacts the Oedipus myth of the lost father and the death of the king. It is articulated out of numerous Biblical tales, and through the expedient of the Bible it becomes a metaphor of race relations in the United States, prohibiting by the very title of the novel a happy ending in the immediate future.

Explicit allusions connect John's condition to that of the American black in general, but the connection is more artificial than organic. But the comparison between Gabriel's behavior and that of the white man does not fail to illuminate the good conscience of the racist (another name for bad faith), although, as we shall see, it is impossible to extend this metaphor to its logical limit within the framework of the novel, a fact which constitutes one of its weaknesses.

John's triumph is the defeat of Gabriel, who sees his fears realized: "Only the son of the bondwoman stood where the rightful heir should stand." (149) Johnny represents the "son of the bondwoman," and the allusion refers to the scene in Genesis in which Sarah demands that Abraham repudiate the son of Hagar the Egyptian. Certain characters correspond to those of the Bible: Gabriel-Abraham, Roy-Isaac, Elizabeth-Hagar, and, finally, Johnny-Ishmael. Ishmael—that is to say the outcast, the Wandering Jew, the accursed. Other pages evoke Gabriel as King David, and Roy his son as Absalom hanged from a tree like a lynched Negro. But above all Gabriel is father Noah, drunk and naked, on whom Ham threw the jeering look of rebellion instead of the cloak of modesty. Johnny-Ham-Ishmael becomes, then, the black son in relation to the white father. And the author insists: "he . . . looked, as the accursed son of Noah had looked, on his father's hideous nakedness," and, six lines later:

> his deadly sin, having looked on his father's nakedness and mocked and cursed him in his heart? Ah, that son of Noah's had been cursed, down to the present groaning generation: *A servant of servants shall he be unto his brethren.* (267)

And he explains almost laboriously:

> All niggers had been cursed, the ironic voice reminded him, all nig-
> gers had come from this most undutiful of Noah's sons. . . . Could
> a curse come down so many ages? (267–268)

The ironic voice of his critical sense frees John from an individual curse (deserved because he has looked on his father's nakedness)
in order to place him under the weight of a collective racial curse,
but in the same movement Baldwin calls into question this religious
pseudo-justification of slavery by a meditation on the reality of
time. Does the fatal charm run through the ages? Does Johnny live
in time or in the moment? In the duration or in the instant? And
is not the instant eternal, out of time, like ecstasy? Thus at the same
time the metaphorical equation of Gabriel = white/John = black is
set up, it is disputed as causality and functions only on the level of
psychological exploration.

In the story of each protagonist, white men do not appear as
fathers but as distant executioners whose blind brutality drives
Richard to suicide, whose domineering sexuality leaves Deborah
ravaged by the side of the road, whose dazzling power renders the
misery of the ghetto all the more dismal. White men do not create,
and when they procreate, they reject the fruit of their sin. The relationship of adulterous father-natural son, Gabriel-Johnny, is metaphorically true. What is more, the American black's history (since
slavery times, which the novel does not fail to evoke briefly) makes
him the natural son of the American white, a son disavowed by his
father. It is precisely here that Gabriel's behavior functions best as
a symbol. Like the white man, he cannot look his own evil full in the
face. Clandestine father of a bastard, he conceals his transgression
so as not to tarnish his image as the leader chosen by the Lord to
propagate the race of the elect. In order to safeguard this good
opinion of himself, he keeps his wickedness at a distance and re-
pudiates it by attributing it to others. By his bad faith, Gabriel
casts a cloud over the life of his own family: he refuses to pardon
Elizabeth's sin; he offers Johnny in expiation of his own transgressions, in a sacrifice that costs him nothing. In addition to the role
of victim (the ugly duckling or the Cinderella of the house), Johnny
has to play, precisely, that of scapegoat (the lamb which replaced
Isaac under the knife just in time). For Johnny is not guilty.
Though a bastard, he is not Gabriel's natural son, and the corre-

spondence does not work in every particular. It remains true only in the mind of the reader (interpreting the novel as a parable, a "fable") to symbolize the bad faith of the white man, who, in order to guard against the sin which eats away at him, transforms the black man into a "Devil's son," into an incarnation of evil identified by his color, stigmatized and branded by all the Biblical symbolism.

This contrast of black and white, shadows and light, extends under the surface of the entire narrative. We point out immediately the immaculate robes of the baptized and the sermons of Gabriel on the theme "I am a man of unclean lips" or Johnny's meditations on "He who is filthy, let him be filthy still." We recall the name of Grimes, or the Sisyphus myth of the child who tries to get out the obstinate and, he knows, unending dirt from the rug. The prisoner of his shame, the black child searches for the reasons of his ostracism as Johnny seeks those of his ugliness. Blackness and ugliness are equivalent in the equation set up by white religion, since scriptural symbolism seems to validate racial prejudice.

Religion, a pretext for the white man, becomes also a "gimmick" for the black man which Robert Bone describes aptly as a "spiritual bleaching cream." [4] Thus the American black calls on the Father Almighty to bestow on him the halo of the golden rays of His Glory. He utilizes religion as a survival tactic. If, for a brief moment, the hero's situation recalls the anguish of the tragic mulatto dear to novelists of the nineteenth century—the bastard who could be redeemed by one word from his Caucasian father—Johnny's existential drama widens rapidly into a parable of the history of black people in the United States, into a chronicle of the means of keeping alive which they have taken from Christianity: Judgment Day, the last shall be first, the son of the bondwoman will stand between God and his father, the legitimate heir of the king being turned against him and his legitimate wife remaining barren. The father does not wish to recognize his bastard, but God will recognize his own. The belief that sustains Johnny as soon as he has accepted his heritage (the negative example of Gabriel, moreover, prohibits him from really rejecting himself) is born of the faith that has sustained black preachers since slavery. It is the dream of a revenge by proxy, of a revenge without that violence which religion condemns. The

4 *The Negro Novel in America,* rev. ed. (New Haven: Yale University Press, 1965), p. 223.

white man believes that his is the chosen race. He belongs, however, to the race of the Pharaohs, not to that of the elect of the Lord,
as the Bible repeats to the black man, who identifies himself with
the Jews of Exodus. The story of Yacub and the mythology of the
Black Muslims reflect the same conviction of belonging to the
chosen race.

Let us go all the way in examining the implications of this racial
metaphor. Does the black man belong, as he believes, to a chosen
people? Yes, Baldwin says, to the extent that he does not yield to
the temptation to throw out on others the instincts which frighten
him, to the exact extent that he is not a Gabriel. That part of his
humanity, of his blackness, of his sin that Johnny takes upon himself, does it not constitute just that "humanity" which the novelist
demands in his essay "Everybody's Protest Novel" that the Afro-
American writer accept?

> "For Bigger's tragedy," Baldwin writes of the hero of *Native Son*,
> "is not that he is cold or black or hungry, not even that he is Amer-
> ican, black; but that he has accepted a theology that denies him life,
> that he admits the possibility of his being sub-human and feels con-
> strained, therefore, to battle for his humanity according to those
> brutal criteria bequeathed him at his birth."

To this point Baldwin seems to suggest that the black man should
reject the definition imposed on him by the white man just as
Johnny refuses that imposed on him by Gabriel, but he goes farther:

> But our humanity is our burden, our life, we need not battle for it;
> we need only do what is infinitely more difficult, that is, accept it.[5]

Such a "humanity" will only be realized by the black man's definition of himself, which implies the acceptance of his negative
aspects. The black man takes on himself the defects of which the
white man tries to unburden himself when he makes the black man
a scapegoat. He becomes a sort of Christ the Redeemer in a perspective that connects the lynching ritual with holy communion.
The black man cannot save himself without saving the white man,
as Baldwin repeats in *The Fire Next Time*. Now the problem is
just that: Johnny cannot save himself without saving Gabriel, and
consequently he does not really save himself at the end of the novel,

---

[5] "Everybody's Protest Novel," *Partisan Review*, 16 (1949), 585.

in spite of that beautiful blaze of mysticism which restores his confidence. Either (and this seems to me to be the case) religion is a "gimmick" which does not provide spiritual salvation, or else it is not a "gimmick" and its efficacious grace redeems everyone. As we have no proof of Gabriel's salvation, Johnny's accordingly remains problematical. *Go Tell It on the Mountain* seems to me to stumble on precisely this point, not only for reasons of psychological motivation, but because the racial metaphor cannot function completely, and above all because the structure of the novel suffers from the same postulate from which it derives its "suspense" and interest. Johnny can assume Gabriel's offenses only if he knows about them, but at no stage of the narrative does he learn what is revealed to the reader: the past of his ancestors, his real derivation, the secret of his stepfather. The racial past, implicit in the protagonist, is not actualized. The converging beams of the destinies of the father, the mother, and the aunt radiate with a brightness focused on this ideal point of conjuncture, the child, but the child is the filament that conveys the light, not the eye that sees it. Transubstantiation does not take place, nor the communion of the saints, and John remains the prisoner of the definition imposed by Gabriel; he does not acquire his adult identity in a true mystical experience. Accordingly, racial conflict cannot be metaphorically resolved within the limits of the narrative. The illumination of the soul is limited to a spark without a future, to a spasm of sensibility in search of love. True knowledge is absent, rebirth impossible.

As dangerous, because partial, as a psychological explanation can appear, I would like here to clarify this check in the functioning of the racial metaphor and, as a result, of the story itself by some consideration of a kind of obstruction that seems to occur in the mind of the novelist. It is not a question of explaining everything, but only of exploring an apparent tendency deep enough to have resulted from a traumatism. And I think that the thin line which separates fiction from autobiography in *Go Tell It on the Mountain* allows us to take this interpretive risk.

The story reflects, barely disguised, Baldwin's own life. The same childhood: David Baldwin, a preacher, in actuality married Emma Berdis Jones three years after James was born, but this stepfather preferred Sam (younger than James), his son by a previous marriage, although this love was not returned. He detested James, on whom devolved the care of the babies who were born after him. His mother's right arm, James was also the ugly duckling of the tale, "frog-eyes" with his large eyes and overlarge mouth which his schoolmates made fun of. He identified himself with Topsy, the gnome of *Uncle Tom's Cabin.* He was a good little student of Public School 24. A white substitute teacher presented him tickets to the World's Fair of 1939. He was the youngster who climbed the hill in Central Park and dreamed of grandeur. He was the one arrested and frisked by the police, shamefully, and the one who mixed hatred for white cops, his stepfather, and his rude schoolmates with an immense, unsatisfied thirst for tenderness, which (just as Johnny becomes a preacher), impelled him to write, not out of a need to distinguish himself, but in order to be loved.

The story of Baldwin's conversion is found in *The Fire Next Time.* At the age of fourteen, James was converted by an evangelist (Margaret in *The Amen Corner,* Praying Mother Elizabeth in the novel) and escaped the wages of sin by entering Calvary Church. He experienced the giddy ecstasy described in "Down at the Cross." He was "saved," both from his father and from Lenox Avenue, because he used religion as an emergency exit. As a holy roller preacher, he asserted during three years a brilliant superiority over his father, and the relations between John and Gabriel retrace those which prevailed between James and David until the death of the latter in 1943.

The writing of *Go Tell It on the Mountain,* then, represents an attempt at liberation for Baldwin. He plunged into it in the same way that he left Harlem for Greenwich Village after his stepfather's death. At the age of eighteen, he had started "Crying Holy," a first fragmentary version, but ten more years were needed for him to assimilate and order his experiences. In 1946, he could read to his friends several chapters of this confession now entitled "In My Father's House." It was then that he met Richard Wright. He had read his books, three profound, dignified, merciless works in which the older man had discovered his identity by opposing the white world. All the respect that one could feel for a literary celebrity separated Baldwin from Wright, but the latter lent a helping hand by recommending the beginner for a Rosenwald Fellowship to his friend Ed Aswell, who was an administrator of the Rosenwald Foundation. This gesture of solidarity did not seem exceptional in Wright's eyes, for he did not pick out Baldwin from among his other protégés. But for the budding novelist, it took on a religious value. It designated him as a writer. It was the kiss of Elisha, the sign of a merciful father who consecrated him. Freed from the paternal image of David, Baldwin immediately set up a new myth by projecting on Wright the image of a spiritual and fraternal father who would recognize his value. The novel-in-progress (to be *Go Tell It on the Mountain*) became the means of being accepted by Wright in the first place. But composition took time, and the writer felt guilty:

> I was ashamed—I thought that I'd done something *terrible* to Richard—because he—he *counted* on me—as I *thought*, y'know, to *do* it. And I'd failed.[6]

The son could be satisfied only if he proved himself worthy of his father—and Baldwin worthy of Wright as a writer.

For the time being, he did not succeed, and it was not his fault. He was cast by the American critical establishment, by editors and literary agents among whom the voice of whites preponderates, into the role of a pugnacious, militant black writer—into the role of Wright. Such was not his vocation at that time. He only wanted to make himself loved and accepted. He was seeking to move the public, whereas Wright struggled to collar the public and force its respect. The former lays claim to affection, the latter to dignity. Their bearing is different, almost opposite, and Baldwin found that others had placed Wright as a sort of obstacle across his natural path, rather similar to his father's blocking his development formerly. "Everyone had always said that Baldwin would be a militant novelist when he grew up, just like Richard Wright," we could say, paraphrasing the first page of the novel. Such seems to be the motive which led Baldwin to write his essay "Everybody's Protest Novel" in 1949, reacting against the point of view of *Uncle Tom's Cabin* but also against the notion of the militant writer which Wright embodied, so that he could claim his right not to be such a writer. For he wanted to conceive racial relations other than as a furious struggle:

> The failure of the protest novel lies in its rejection of life, the human being, the denial of his beauty, dread, power, in its insistence

[6] Fern Marja Eckman, *The Furious Passage of James Baldwin* (New York: M. Evans, 1966), p. 105.

that it is his categorization alone which is real and which cannot be transcended.[7]

By this general declaration, Baldwin demanded first of all the freedom to write according to his understanding. But what happens in Baldwin's mind remained strange to Wright's. Wright did not understand that Baldwin needed his "paternity" in order to succeed and that the critical essays of the perplexed young man were trying, in effect, to compel him to grant his friendship to him. Wright had caused to be published in *Zero* the very essay by Baldwin that brought Wright into the matter, and he was astonished by Baldwin's attack. He kept his distance and refused a deeper friendship. Meanwhile, apparently freed by this definition of self, Baldwin had reoriented his style, his writing, his art. He was now able to finish his novel in three months. At Loches-les-Bains, near Lausanne, his friend Lucien Happersberger opened his family chalet to him, and on February 26, 1952, Baldwin literally descended from the mountain to mail the manuscript of *Go Tell It on the Mountain*.

The sequel to the Wright-Baldwin relationship is in the domain of minor literary history, but it is important to know it in order to understand Baldwin's ulterior behavior. He was continuing the effort to destroy his father-idol, and as one could expect, his final victory only brought him unhappiness. This friendship which might have flourished remained for Baldwin a story of disappointed love, and we think once more of Johnny:

> Oh, that his father would *die!*—and the road before John be open, as it must be open for others. Yet in the very grave he would hate him; his father would but have changed conditions, he would be John's father still. (195)

It is tempting to see, insinuating itself in the very woof of the novel in composition, the thread of this ambiguous and unbalanced relationship which was established between the two writers in 1952, this story of an unsuccessful encounter. Deeply provoked by this humble and undignified quest for his affection, Wright refused his friendship. Baldwin took this refusal as a matter of pride or jealousy over his literary success. Soon his articles on the meetings of the Franco-American Fellowship in 1951 or the First Congress of Black Writers and Artists at the Sorbonne in September 1956 pre-

[7] "Everybody's Protest Novel," p. 585.

sented Wright as a person who needed to feel superior. Because he suffered from not having been recognized by Wright when others, like Chester Himes, were Wright's friends in exile, Baldwin went as far as partially to invent the story of a happy evening when Wright, Himes, and he met again on equal footing, without problems, in a Parisian cafe. We should read this as the projection of a dream of reconciliation rather than as the description of a harmony that had never existed. Afterwards this feeling turned sour, and Baldwin seemed to lend himself to maneuvers intended to demolish the statue—now too cumbersome—which American criticism had formerly erected of Wright. It was not careerism, I believe, that then impelled Baldwin to intrigue for reports about Wright in Mr. Luce's magazines. It was rather a kind of psychological fatality comparable to the struggle for life he had made with his stepfather, a deep need to supplant the spiritual father whom he had chosen and who had rejected him. A strange situation, since it was Baldwin himself who had placed Wright in this role without his consent! When the older man died in November 1960, the novelist was finally free to become himself. For to the extent that he has grown up, he has been able to do without acceptance, and his work has become more militant, more cutting, nearer in a word to the committed literature which he criticized in 1950.

Certainly his work has never lost its sentimental tones, its ambience both homosexual and religious (the homosexual, after all, is the priest, such as Elisha symbolizes), but it came to shape itself according to the state of mind of black people, whose spokesman Baldwin became during the great civil rights campaigns. In 1960 he experienced no more difficulty in putting on Wright's shoes as a committed writer than he previously had in wearing the preacher's shoes of David Baldwin. His political evolution coincides with a profound psychological evolution, the one illuminating the other. He became a militant writer on civil rights after the fashion of the spiritual father that he had chosen.

One can deplore the initial misunderstanding that separated the two novelists. Baldwin would certainly have been contented with a friendship in which he did not have the principal role. His ambition was less great than his desire to be accepted by Wright. One can deplore the meanness which impelled him to give a donkey's kick to the dead lion in "Alas, Poor Richard." But this reaction should be understood, it seems to me, as a gesture of despair and impotence. Wright, after his death, had become the father who would never recognize the one who wished to be his son. As it had been necessary to destroy him while he was alive because he constituted an obstacle to his development, now Baldwin seemed to wish to destroy the dead man in order to efface the eternal regret of a friendship which could have been realized.[8] This attitude, called up in the controversy between Irving Howe and Ralph Ellison [see page 97 this volume] over black protest literature,[9] derives less in Baldwin from a theoretical position than from an emotional reaction. It is not the expression of a man who fights for his ideas, but the sentimental reaction, sometimes almost pathological, of a wounded nature.

Since *Go Tell It on the Mountain* Baldwin has seemed determined to remain an Ishmael in search of a father or, in the absence of a father, an adopted brother. Such is the central, traumatic reaction that the writer's behavior repeats and betrays, which his writing itself echoes, more with a therapeutic end than in a conscious desire to exploit the material in literature. Without wishing to reduce the man to this sole relationship, without trying to interpret too reductively a novel that casts light on all aspects of the world of religion, sexuality, and interracial relations, it seems to me impossible not to consider this father-son relationship as primary. At this stage the novel runs the risk of seeming to be not so much another literary production as another type of "gimmick," a stratagem for survival similar to religion, a system for projecting the fantasies that have haunted the "bastard" son since childhood. From this fact comes the work's profound autobiographical resonance, as well as its limitations, perhaps. But the greatness of the work and its incontestable literary value perhaps arise from the fact that this drama of the search for a father is not limited to the form taken by a traumatism. It lends itself admirably to a metaphorical exploitation because it unites itself quite naturally with one of the fundamental archetypes of human history.

[8] Baldwin says this honestly, after all, in "The Exile," in *Nobody Knows My Name* (New York: The Dial Press, 1961), pp. 190–199.

[9] See Irving Howe, "Black Boys and Native Sons," *Dissent*, 10 (1963), 353–368, and Ralph Ellison, "The World and the Jug," in *Shadow and Act* (New York: Random House, 1964), pp. 107–143.

"Sonny's Blues": James Baldwin's Image of Black Community

by John M. Reilly

A critical commonplace holds that James Baldwin writes better essays than he does fiction or drama; nevertheless, his leading theme —the discovery of identity—is nowhere presented more successfully than in the short story "Sonny's Blues." Originally published in *Partisan Review* in 1957 and reprinted in the collection of stories *Going to Meet the Man* in 1965, "Sonny's Blues" not only states dramatically the motive for Baldwin's famous polemics in the cause of Black freedom, but it also provides an esthetic linking his work, in all literary genres, with the cultures of the Black ghetto.[1]

The fundamental movement of "Sonny's Blues" represents the slow accommodation of a first-person narrator's consciousness to the meaning of his younger brother's way of life. The process leads Baldwin's readers to a sympathetic engagement with the young man by providing a knowledge of the human motives of the youths whose lives normally are reported to others only by their inclusion in statistics of school dropout rates, drug usage, and unemployment.

The basis of the story, however, and its relationship to the purpose of Baldwin's writing generally, lies in his use of the Blues as a key metaphor. The unique quality of the Blues is its combination of personal and social significance in a lyric encounter with history. "The Blues-singer describes first-person experiences, but only such as are typical of the community and such as each individual in the community might have. The singer never sets himself against the

[1] *Partisan Review*, XXIV (Summer, 1957), 327–58. *Going to Meet the Man* (New York, 1965), pp. 103–41. Citations in the text are from the latter publication of the story.

community or raises himself above it." [2] Thus, in the story of Sonny and his brother an intuition of the meaning of the Blues repairs the relationship between the two men who have chosen different ways to cope with the meanacing ghetto environment, and their reconciliation through the medium of this Afro-American musical form extends the meaning of the individual's Blues until it becomes a metaphor of Black community.

Sonny's life explodes into his older brother's awareness when the story of his arrest for peddling and using heroin is reported in the newspaper. Significantly the mass medium of the newspaper with the impersonal story in it of a police bust is the only way the brothers have of communicating at the opening of the story. While the narrator says that because of the newspaper report Sonny "became real to me again," their relationship is only vestigially personal, for he "couldn't find any room" for the news "anywhere inside . . ." (103).

While he had had his suspicions about how Sonny was spending his life, the narrator had put them aside with rationalizations about how Sonny was, after all, a good kid. Nothing to worry about. In short, the storyteller reveals that along with his respectable job as an algebra teacher he had assumed a conventional way of thinking as a defense against recognizing that his own brother ran the risk of "coming to nothing." Provoked by the facts of Sonny's arrest to observe his students, since they are the same age as Sonny must have been when he first had heroin, he notices for the first time that their laughter is disenchanted rather than good-humored. In it he hears his brother, and perhaps himself. At this point in the story his opinion is evidently that Sonny and many of the young students are beaten and he, fortunately, is not.

The conventionality of the narrator's attitude becomes clearer when he encounters a nameless friend of Sonny's, a boy from the block who fears he may have touted Sonny onto heroin by telling him, truthfully, how great it made him feel to be high. This man who "still spent hours on the street corner . . . high and raggy" explains what will happen to Sonny because of his arrest. After they send him someplace and try to cure him, they'll let Sonny loose, that's all. Trying to grasp the implication the narrator asks: "You mean he'll never kick the habit. Is that what you mean?" He feels

    [2] Janheinz Jahn, *Neo-African Literature: A History of Black Writing* (New York, 1968), p. 166.

there should be some kind of renewal, some hope. A man should be able to bring himself up by his will, convention says. Convention also says that behavior like Sonny's is deliberately self-destructive. "Tell me," he asks the friend, "why does he want to die?" Wrong again. "Don't nobody want to die," says the friend, "ever" (108).

Agitated though he is about Sonny's fate the narrator doesn't want to feel himself involved. His own position on the middle-class ladder of success is not secure, and the supporting patterns of thought in his mind are actually rather weak. Listening to the nameless friend explain about Sonny while they stand together in front of a bar blasting "black and bouncy" music from its door, he senses something that frightens him. "All this was carrying me some place I didn't want to go. I certainly didn't want to know how it felt. It filled everything, the people, the houses, the music, the dark, quicksilver barmaid, with menace; and this menace was their reality" (107).

Eventually a great personal pain—the loss of a young daughter—breaks through the narrator's defenses and makes him seek out his brother, more for his own comfort than for Sonny's. "My trouble made his real," he says. In that remark is a prefiguring of the meaning the Blues will develop.

It is only a prefiguring, however, for the time Sonny is released from the state institution where he had been confined, the narrator's immediate need for comfort has passed. When he meets Sonny he is in control of himself, but very shortly he is flooded with complex feelings that make him feel again the menace of the 110th Street bar where he had stood with Sonny's friend. There is no escaping a feeling of icy dread, so he must try to understand.

As the narrator casts his mind back over his and Sonny's past, he gradually identifies sources of his feelings. First he recalls their parents, especially concentrating on an image of his family on a typical Sunday. The scene is one of security amidst portentousness. The adults sit without talking, "but every face looks darkening, like the sky outside." The children sit about, maybe one half asleep and another being stroked on the head by an adult. The darkness frightens a child and he hopes "that the hand which strokes his forehead will never stop." The child knows, however, that it will end, and now grown-up he recalls one of the meanings of the darkness is in the story his mother told him of the death of his uncle, run over on a dark country road by a car full of drunken white men. Never had his companion, the boy's father, "seen anything as dark as that road after the lights of the car had gone away." The narrator's mother had attempted to apply her tale of his father's grief at the death of his own brother to the needs of their sons. They can't protect each other, she knows, "but," she says to the narrator about Sonny, "you got to let him know you's *there*" (119).

Thus, guilt for not fulfilling their mother's request and a sense of shared loneliness partially explain the older brother's feeling toward Sonny. Once again, however, Baldwin stresses the place of the conventional set of the narrator's mind in the complex of feelings as he has him recall scenes from the time when Sonny had started to become a jazz musician. The possibility of Sonny's being a jazz rather than a classical musician had "seemed—beneath him, somehow." Trying to understand the ambition, the narrator had asked if Sonny meant to play like Louis Armstrong, only to be told that Charlie Parker was the model. Hard as it is to believe, he had never heard of Bird until Sonny mentioned him. This ignorance reveals more than a gap between fraternal generations. It represents a cultural chasm. The narrator's inability to understand Sonny's choice of a musical leader shows his alienation from the mood of the post-war bebop sub-culture. In its hip style of dress, its repudiation of middle-brow norms, and its celebration of esoteric manner the bebop sub-culture made overtly evident its underlying significance as an assertion of Black identity. Building upon a restatement of Afro-American music, bebop became an expression of a new self-awareness in the ghettos by a strategy of elaborate non-conformity. In committing himself to the bebop sub-culture Sonny attempted to make a virtue of the necessity of the isolation imposed upon him by his color. In contrast, the narrator's failure to understand what Sonny was doing indicates that his response to the conditions imposed upon him by racial status was to try to assimilate himself as well as he could into the mainstream American culture. For the one, heroin addiction sealed his membership in the exclusive group; for the other, adoption of individualistic attitudes marked his allegiance to the historically familiar ideal of transcending caste distinctions by entering into the middle class.

Following his way Sonny became wrapped in the vision that rose from his piano, stopped attending school, and hung around with a group of musicians in Greenwich Village. His musical friends became Sonny's family, replacing the brother who had felt that

Sonny's choice of his style of life was the same thing as dying, and for all practical purposes the brothers were dead to each other in the extended separation before Sonny's arrest on narcotics charges.

The thoughts revealing the brothers' family history and locating the sources of the narrator's complex feelings about Sonny all occur in the period after Sonny is released from the state institution. Though he has ceased to evade thoughts of their relationship, as he had done in the years when they were separated and had partially continued to do after Sonny's arrest, the narrator has a way to go before he can become reconciled to Sonny. His recollections of the past only provide his consciousness with raw feeling.

The next development—perception—begins with a scene of a revival meeting conducted on the sidewalk of Seventh Avenue, beneath the narrator's window. Everyone on the street has been watching such meetings all his life, but the narrator from his window, passersby on the street, and Sonny from the edge of the crowd all watch again. It isn't because they expect something different this time. Rather it is a familiar moment of communion for them. In basic humanity one of the sanctified sisters resembles the down-and-outer watching her, "a cigarette between her heavy, chapped lips, her hair a cuckoo's nest, her face scarred and swollen from many beatings. . . . Perhaps," the narrator thinks, "they both knew this, which was why, when, as rarely, they addressed each other, they addressed each other as Sister" (129). The point impresses both the narrator and Sonny, men who should call one another "Brother," for the music of the revivalists seems to "soothe a poison" out of them.

The perception of this moment extends nearly to conception in the conversation between the narrator and Sonny that follows it. It isn't a comfortable discussion. The narrator still is inclined to voice moral judgments of the experiences and people Sonny tries to talk about, but he is making an honest effort to relate to his brother now and reminds himself to be quiet and listen. What he hears is that Sonny equates the feeling of hearing the revivalist sister sing with the sensation of heroin in the veins. "It makes you feel—in control. Sometimes you got to have that feeling" (131). It isn't primarily drugs that Sonny is talking about, though, and when the narrator curbs his tongue to let him go on, Sonny explains the real subject of his thoughts.

Again, the facts of Sonny's experience contradict the opinion of "respectable" people. He did not use drugs to escape from suffering, he says. He knows as well as anyone that there's no way to avoid suffering, but what you can do is "try all kinds of ways to keep from drowning in it, to keep on top of it, and to make it seem . . . like *you.*" That is, Sonny explains, you can earn your suffering, make it seem "like you did something . . . and now you're suffering for it" (132).

The idea of meriting your suffering is a staggering one. In the face of it the narrator's inclination to talk about "will power and how life could be—well, beautiful," is blunted, because he senses that by directly confronting degradation Sonny has asserted what degree of will was possible to him, and perhaps that kept him alive.

At this point in the story it is clear that there are two themes emerging. The first is the theme of the individualistic narrator's gradual discovery of the significance of his brother's life. This theme moves to a climax in the final scene of the story when Sonny's music impresses the narrator with a sense of the profound feeling it contains. From the perspective of that final scene, however, the significance of the Blues itself becomes a powerful theme.

The insight into suffering that Sonny displays establishes his priority in knowledge. Thus, he reverses the original relationship between the brothers, assumes the role of the elder, and proceeds to lead his brother, by means of the Blues, to a discovery of self in community.

As the brothers enter the jazz club where Sonny is to play, he becomes special. Everyone has been waiting for him, and each greets him familiarly. Equally special is the setting—dark except for a spotlight which the musicians approach as if it were a circle of flame. This is a sanctified spot where Sonny is to testify to the power of souls to commune in the Blues.

Baldwin explicates the formula of the Blues by tracing the narrator's thoughts while Sonny plays. Many people, he thinks, don't really hear music being played except so far as they invest it with "personal, private, vanishing evocations." He might be thinking of himself, referring to his having come to think of Sonny through the suffering of his own personal loss. The man who makes the music engages in a spiritual creation, and when he succeeds, the creation belongs to all present, "his triumph, when he triumphs, is ours" (137).

In the first set Sonny doesn't triumph, but in the second, appropriately begun by "Am I Blue," he takes the lead and begins to form a musical creation. He becomes, in the narrator's words, "part of the family again" (139). What family? First of all that of his fellow musicians. Then, of course, the narrator means to say that their fraternal relationship is at last fulfilled as their mother hoped it to be. But there is yet a broader meaning too. Like the sisters at the Seventh Avenue revival meeting Sonny and the band are not saying anything new. Still they are keeping the Blues alive by expanding it beyond the personal lyric into a statement of the glorious capacity of human beings to take the worst and give it a form of their own. choosing.

At this point the narrator synthesizes feelings and perception into a conception of the Blues. He realizes Sonny's Blues can help everyone who listens be free, in his own case free of the conventions that had alienated him from Sonny and that dimension of Black culture represented in Sonny's style of living. Yet at the same time he knows the world outside of the Blues moment remains hostile.

The implicit statement of the esthetics of the Blues in this story throws light upon much of Baldwin's writing. The first proposition of the esthetics that we can infer from "Sonny's Blues" is that suffering is the prior necessity. Integrity of expression comes from "paying your dues." This is a point Baldwin previously made in *Giovanni's Room* (1956) and which he elaborated in the novel *Another Country* (1962).

The second implicit proposition of the Blues esthetics is that while the form is what it's all about, the form is transitory. The Blues is an art in process and in that respect alien from any conception of fixed and ideal forms. This will not justify weaknesses in an artist's work, but insofar as Baldwin identifies his writing with the art of the singers of Blues it suggests why he is devoted to representation, in whatever genre, of successive moments of expressive feeling and comparatively less concerned with achieving a consistent overall structure.

The final proposition of the esthetic in the story "Sonny's Blues" is that the Blues functions as an art of communion. It is popular rather than elite, worldly rather than otherwise. The Blues is expression in which one uses the skill he has achieved by practice and experience in order to reach toward others. It is this proposition that gives the Blues its metaphoric significance. The fraternal reconciliation brought about through Sonny's music is emblematic of a group's coming together, because the narrator learns to love his brother freely while he discovers the value of a characteristically Afro-American assertion of life-force. Taking Sonny on his own terms he must also abandon the ways of thought identified with middle-class position which historically has signified for Black people the adoption of "white" ways.

An outstanding quality of the Black literary tradition in America is its attention to the interdependence of personal and social experience. Obviously necessity has fostered this virtue. Black authors cannot luxuriate in the assumption that there is such a thing as a purely private life. James Baldwin significantly adds to this aspect of the tradition in "Sonny's Blues" by showing that artful expression of personal yet typical experience is one way to freedom.

The Black Musician:
The Black Hero as Light Bearer

by Sherley Anne Williams

The musician in the works of James Baldwin is more than a metaphor; he is the embodiment of alienation and estrangement, which the figure of the artist becomes in much of twentieth century literature. Most of his characters have at the center of their portrayal an isolation from the society, the culture, even each other. They are also commentaries upon the brutal, emasculating, feared —and fearing—land from which they are so estranged. The musician is also for Baldwin an archetypal figure whose referent is Black lives, Black experiences and Black deaths. He is the hope of making it in America and the bitter mockery of never making it well enough to escape the danger of being Black, the living symbol of alienation from the past and hence from self and the rhythmical link with the mysterious ancestral past. That past and its pain and the transcendence of pain is always an implicit part of the musician's characterization in Baldwin. Music is the medium through which the musician achieves enough understanding and strength to deal with the past and present hurt.

The short story, "Sonny's Blues," sketches this kind of relationship between the individual and his personal and group history. Sonny is a jazz pianist who has recently returned from a drug cure. The story is set in New York, Harlem, and seems at first glance merely another well-written story about a young Black man trying to become himself, to attain his majority and retain his humanity amid all the traps which have been set to prevent just that. But the simplicity of the tale is only surface deep; in a rising crescendo of

"The Black Musician: The Black Hero as Light Bearer" by Sherley Anne Williams. From *Give Birth to Brightness* (New York: The Dial Press, 1972), pp. 145–66, the original material by Sherley Anne Williams only. Copyright © 1972 by Sherley Anne Williams. Reprinted by permission of The Dial Press.

thematic complexity, the present struggle is refracted through the age-old pain, the age-old life force. The story is narrated by Sonny's older brother who has found it difficult to understand what music means to Sonny. Sonny's desire to be a jazz musician, which his brother associates with the "good-time" life, has created a schism between himself and his more orthodox brother. And because the brother cannot understand what lies between himself and Sonny, he cannot forgive Sonny for Sonny's own pain, which he, for all his seniority, is powerless to ease, or for the pain which their ruptured relationship has caused him. The closing pages of the story are a description of the brother's reaction as he listens to Sonny play for the first time. . . .

The attempt to once again make it through music brings no instant transformation. Sonny is approaching the center of his life and he cannot know what he will find there. But he understands that if he is to live, he must deal with that dread, that terror, chance the terrifying in order to triumph. . . .

The musical group, Ellison's "marvel of social organization,"[1] is the catalyst which makes it possible for Sonny to begin to see himself through the music, to play out his own pain through the expression of it. . . .

Sonny's music and his life become one and he is fused with the musical group in a relationship which sustains one because it sustains all. And finally, through the music, Sonny's brother begins to understand not so much Sonny, as himself, *his* past, *his* history, *his* traditions and that part of himself which he has in common with Sonny and the long line of people who have gone before them. . . .

It is this then, this intense, almost excruciating, but always sustaining relationship among musicians and between them and their audiences which the musician is meant to evoke. The emphasis is gradually transformed from pain to survival to life. All are linked together by invisible webs, indestructible bonds of tradition and history, and this heritage, once revealed, becomes the necessary regenerative power which makes life possible. One senses this in Rufus, the drummer and central character in the first Book of *Another Country*. . . . But this relationship is subverted and eventually destroyed by Rufus's involvement with a Southern white woman, Leona, a poor, plain girl-woman whom Baldwin seems to

1 Ralph Ellison, "Living with Music," *Shadow and Act* (New York: New American Library, 1964), p. 189.

posit as one part of the reality behind the myth of sacred Southern white womanhood. But in grappling with her, Rufus is hedged about by the brutality of the past and his own slender personal resources. The integration of past and present is always on the level of pain and never that of life. The strength which made it possible for his ancestors to endure and to survive that pain is buried somewhere within Rufus, in a place which he does not even realize exists. He becomes more entangled with Leona, wallowing in an ancient source of pain, but never calls upon his family, or his music, the symbols of life, the talismen against death which might have been his salvation—and Leona's. He attempts to use sex as a weapon against her in the same way in which white society has used sex as a weapon against him. The "terrible muscle" and the "violent deep," the male and female sexual organs in Baldwin's works, are always, when used as weapons, self-destructive. Leona is driven insane by Rufus's brutal treatment of her. Rufus, weighted down with guilt and the pain of both past and present, commits suicide.

Baldwin attempts to establish a contrasting structure between this relationship and the relationship which develops between Vivaldo, the white boy who had been his best friend, and Ida, his beloved younger sister. Rufus and Leona end their lives in despair and death, while Vivaldo and Ida, drawn together at first by the love they both had for Rufus, finally achieve an uneasy peace with each other. It is a peace, which, though hard won and perhaps easily lost, is based on a deeper understanding of themselves and each other and their relationship. Rufus returns to the past and cannot find his way out again. But Vivaldo, in his relationship with Ida, tries to move into the future, to break the mold of degradation and humiliation which has usually characterized the relationship of white men with Black women.

Rufus's struggle informs the other two Books in the novel, and the characters are defined and distinguished through their relationship to him. The strength of the first Book, however, its technical and thematic brilliance, finds only dim echoes in these later portions and it is the agony of Rufus as he seeks to reconcile the past hate with the present love and his tragic failure which dominates the novel.

In *Blues for Mister Charlie,* the outline sketched in "Sonny's Blues" becomes a tumultuous and vivid portrayal of that history and tradition which has made Black experience Black life. Richard has lost touch with the group, abused himself and his tradition and fallen back on drugs as a means of making it through the world. Because of his drug thing, he is out of step, out of time and the play, in part, deals with Richard's attempt to get back in step, to find that lost group rhythm.

II

The coming together of the group and the individual, of Richard and the Black chorus, in *Blues for Mister Charlie* is sparked by Juanita, the young woman whom he comes to love and who loves him. But the union takes place on a level which seems to have been too subtle for most reviewers to note. Typical of these analyses is Edward Margolies' comment that Richard is "highly neurotic, obstreperous, and disagreeable." Margolies sees Richard's only claim to heroism, "if," as he carefully modifies it, "it can be called that," as Richard's "ability to articulate all the venom and bitterness he feels toward whites. It is an act of courage, but there is little else about him that is admirable." [2] Margolies has perhaps been overcome by Baldwin's scathing indictment of white people. While one would certainly not want to stop Baldwin from indicting all the white people he wants, one of the central concerns of the play, the growth of Richard, is likely to be overlooked as Black audiences applaud, Right on! and white audiences squirm and cry, Not so! The indictment of racism is merely a backdrop for the character of Richard and all he represents as musician and Black man.

The action of *Blues for Mister Charlie* centers around the return of Richard to his home in a small Southern town. Richard runs afoul of one of the town's most notorious racists, who murders him. The murderer, Lyle Britten, is tried by an all-white jury and acquitted. The atmosphere of the play is dominated, in part, by a white chorus whose movements are the stylized motions of not very lifelike dolls. The mechanical quality is intentional and the motions and emotions of the white town rise to an almost sexual climax during the third act courtroom scenes where the chorus attempts to castrate and/or impale Black witnesses on the spikes of their own sexual fears. Lyle, the murderer, Jo, his wife, and Parnell, the liberal, would-be friend of white and Black stand out against the

2 Edward Margolies, *Native Sons* (Philadelphia: J. B. Lippincott, 1968), p. 125.

chorus, not because they are different, but because they are heightened, more humanized forms of the fears and repressions, hopes, loves and lusts of the whitetown chorus.

On the other side of the street, literally, is the Black chorus, seemingly drawn in different directions but united in the need to win free of the yoke of oppression whose reins are held by whitetown. There is fury and rage in them, but also tenderness and a painful driving energy which struggles for release in Richard, Meridian, his father, and Juanita. The third act brings the Blacktown chorus no release, no climax, for though their presence has helped the Black witnesses resist the repeated attempts to humiliate and degrade them, the courtroom verdict is no more than they expected. It merely confirms the necessity of finding a release for the fury which Richard's death has intensified.

Richard is a musician, a singer, and the first time he is evoked in the play as a person it is through his songs. . . . But it is not so much the "man" whom Richard is in trouble with, as with himself. The audience first sees him standing in his room singing, so that one is made aware from the start of the frantic power and the glory, too, of Richard the artist. . . .

Richard left the South during his adolescence compelled by the outside force of his father's need to save him from growing up in the town which, perhaps literally, had killed Richard's mother and impelled by his own inner sense of his father's powerlessness before the white world. His father could not even protect his mother and Richard sees himself in his father's lack of power. But Richard finds in the ambiguities of the North—ambiguities which are no more than masks for the same pathological race attitudes from which he fled—no solace, no peace. . . .

In Richard's first scenes, his knowledge of his own weakness, and the weakness of Black men, is patent. He acknowledges his own helplessness and the Black man's inability to protect his woman, and then, immediately, partly to bolster his own ego, partly to make up in sexuality what he lacks in power, he speaks of his conquest of white women. . . .

Juanita sees through this device, sees the sadness behind his bravado, sees that Richard's use of white women is finally no more than an outlet for the thwarted rage he feels for white society and, most particularly, for white men. For Richard, crippled by his sense of weakness, has to parade his sexuality because he feels it is the one thing he has left which makes him a man. And when even this pretended power loses its effectiveness, he turns to drugs. . . .

But even cured of drugs he must still brag of his potency before Juanita, before Pete, before Lyle Britten and it is only when he realizes that another beautiful person sees his beauty and will respond to it and care for him, that he no longer needs to brag, no longer needs to issue challenges. . . . He understands his father and something of what his father has gone through, has had to live. And he is now able to tuck his past, and that of his father's and his father's father, around him like an old but loved cloak, for remembering brings not only pain but strength and selfhood.

His newly found selfhood, however, is a challenge in itself, for it means that others must now relate to him in a new way. Even Lyle Britten's dogged need to prove his masculinity at Richard's expense does not shake Richard's newly defined self. Thus it is that the wild challenge, the almost hysterical taunting which characterized his first confrontation with Lyle, is absent from his death scene. Here, Richard wants only to be left alone, to disengage himself from the society which had made it necessary for him to use white women and drugs in order to feel that he existed. . . . But Lyle, the white man, refuses to admit that he has even heard what is a request from one man to another. And Richard is forced to school him, to speak to Lyle as one would to a young and not very much loved child. Speaking in the collective voice of Black men, he lays bare the phoniness, the fakery, at the root of Lyle's masculinity and dignity. . . . Sex is a metaphor for power but the power which it symbolizes is a sham, a façade behind which lurks the weakness of those—both white and Black—who would use it as an instrument of subjugation or oppression. Baldwin implies that this is the great tragedy of white people, that sex is for them only a means of claiming, of dominating others, that there is all take and very little give in their relationships. There is, as Juanita remarks of Parnell, no flesh they can really touch. Or, it is like Parnell's play on words, "peace" and "piece" in the third act. Peace is union with a citadel, a Jo Britten, to whom the mind is a citadel from which all thoughts of sexuality must be chased. She thinks, instead, of possessions and material things. Marriage becomes nothing more than an escape from the fear of having "to spend the rest of [her] life serving coffee to strangers in church basements." Peace is something divorced from heat or warmth and it is indeed a very sobering thought, while "piece" is "poontang," the debased but life-giving fire of a Black woman. In acquiring, in mastering, both the "peace" and the "piece" the white man proves anew, with his penis, now, instead of his whip or his money or his law, his superiority over the Black man. Lyle, the poor white man, puts the two together and builds his life on this and when Richard tells him by his actions that both his citadel and his poontang are mere imitations of the reality which he, Richard, possesses, Lyle kills him, for Richard has threatened his very life.

Parnell, the rich liberal, is Lyle's best friend, his other, thinking half. He sees quite clearly the willful self-delusions at the basis of Lyle's life and his own. . . . He is drawn to the other side of town by its vitality, its regenerative strength. But the feeling that there must be something depraved, unclean about life in the midst of so much squalor and tragedy persists. . . . And finally he is thrown back upon the aridness, the paucity of soul force in his own life. . . .

And just as clearly, Richard moves beyond Parnell's vision, can, in fact, no longer be touched by it. He comes full circle and the unity of experience which was sundered by his mother's death is renewed by Juanita's life and love. The idea of a circular movement is reinforced on a more obvious level by the fact that Richard and Juanita were childhood friends, almost sweethearts, and had Richard remained in their hometown, they, as he remarks to Meridian, would probably have been married and have a couple of kids.

As it is, the two of them bring another kind of awareness to their renewed relationship. Richard has been down the road a little and Juanita has remained fecund, waiting, unconsciously, for the touch which is Richard's. She questions him about his "illness" not out of curiosity but out of concern. . . . And Richard, sensing that this may not be "one of those times," returns to the idea, testing it, "So you care about me, do you? Ain't that a bitch?" for he finds it hard to believe that someone can.

In a richly evocative scene, Juanita broaches the idea of their going through the world together. . . . At exactly what point Richard begins to believe that Juanita can and does care about him is not important. What is important is that he does come to believe and it is this belief which reinforces his sense of identity, and his "I know I can do it. I know I can do it" refers not so much to the knowledge that he can ask Juanita to marry him, that he can take her away with him, as it does to the knowledge that he can take care of her and protect her as his father had not been able to care for or protect his mother.

Richard is linked to the blacktown chorus by the color of his skin and through the common roots of their history and experience. Through his relationship with Juanita, the link, despite his death, remains concrete and alive, for if loving Juanita makes a man of Richard, he makes a woman of her. . . . Or again, as she tells Parnell before Lyle Britten's trial, "One day. I'll recover [from the pain of Richard's death]. I'm sure that I'll recover. And I'll see the world again—the marvelous world. And I'll have learned from Richard—how to love." This is spoken in the comparative calm after the shock and pain of Richard's death have eased somewhat. But even in the wildness of grief, enough of Richard's grace—for there is no other word to describe the power and beauty which characterize Richard in those last moments of his life—clings to Juanita so that she can acknowledge that the long lines of Black people brought to fruition in her and in Richard does not stop in her body or end in Richard's death. . . .

If there is no compassion, no sympathy for Parnell in this brief acknowledgment, there is the awareness that Parnell's barrenness and, perhaps, that of whites has somehow touched and stained Black people. The focus here, however, has changed from castigating those who have touched them, as Richard does earlier in the play—to how they may free themselves from the barrenness of those touches. Thus, when Juanita acquiesces to Parnell's request to accompany her and the blacktown chorus to the church at the end of the play, it is out of a sense of her own hard-won selfhood and womanhood and the knowledge that easing her own pain does not necessarily mean causing pain to others. Her action does not absolve him of his complicity in Lyle's acquittal, nor is it meant to; rather, it removes Parnell to the outer fringe of her life as she joins with blacktown in the problem of getting on with Black life.

Richard sees the group tradition as weak, powerless. He seeks to define himself in opposition to it as powerful, a conqueror. It is only when he discovers that pain endured in seeming docility and passivity does not need to be a source of humiliation and continuing shame, that he can draw on the life-giving force represented by that experience. He learns that he need not fear pain, for he and his people have been there before; having made it through once, they can make it through again.

James Baldwin on the Sixties:
Acts and Revelations

by Benjamin DeMott

Pity spokesmen; their lot is hard. The movement of their ideas is looked at differently from that of other men, studied for clues and confirmations, and comes therefore to seem unindividual—less a result of personal growth than of cultural upsurge. Why in 1961 did James Baldwin speak of the black man's "love" of the white man? (The passage occurs in *Notes of a Native Son*: "No one in the world . . . knows Americans better or . . . loves them more than the American Negro. . . . We are bound together forever. We are part of each other.") Answer: Baldwin spoke of love because the times dictated this line.

Again, why in 1963 did James Baldwin amend the concept of love, introducing the notion of a saving remnant committed to raising levels of consciousness? (The passage occurs at the end of *The Fire Next Time*: "If we—and now I mean the relatively conscious whites and the relatively conscious blacks, who must, like lovers, insist on, or create, the consciousness of the others—do not falter in our duty now, we may be able, handful that we are, to end racial nightmare, and achieve our country, and change the history of the world.") Answer: Baldwin amended the concept of love because in those years the movement had begun to awaken to itself and the awakening dictated the amendments.

Yet again, why in 1972 does James Baldwin announce that the black man "must kill" the white? (The passages occur in the book at hand: ". . . it is not necessary for a black man to hate a white man, or to have any particular feelings about him at all, in order to realize that he must kill him." And, "There will be bloody hold-

"James Baldwin on the Sixties: Acts and Revelations" by Benjamin DeMott. First appeared in *Saturday Review*, May 27, 1972. Used with permission of the publisher.

ing actions all over the world, for years to come: but the Western party is over, and the white man's sun has set. Period.") Answer: Baldwin speaks of killing because the advent of a new militancy, together with disillusionment about prospects for reform, dictates still further change.

Difficulty in seeming to be your own man, rather than a knee-jerk reactor to events, is but one of many problems besetting spokesmen. Another has to do with expense of spirit. Few Americans have been called on as frequently as has James Baldwin in the last decade to function as the public voice of rage or frustration or denunciation or grief. Repeatedly, on television, on college platforms, at hundreds of public meetings, the author of *The Fire Next Time* has had to seek within himself both the energies and the vocabulary of fury—to search for the words that will make real to himself and others the latest atrocity. Traditional oratory can perhaps be equal to cattle prods, mortgage racketeers, heroin syndicates, and assassinations. But where in his word-hoard can a spokesman reach for means of articulating feelings about defenseless children bombed to death while singing a hymn at Sunday school? What terms does he find to name his revulsion on learning that at a state prison an already wounded prisoner was stabbed three times in the rectum with a screwdriver by a "correction officer"? How does he conduct a hunt for language that hasn't been emptied out by repetition—how can he witness his own scramblings for freshness without coming in some sense to despise this self-involved fastidiousness? To function as a voice of outrage month after month for a decade and more strains heart and mind, and rhetoric as well; the consequence is a writing style ever on the edge of being winded by too many summonses to intensity. You write, if you are James Baldwin, "The land seems nearly to weep beneath the burden of this civilization's unnameable excrescences"—and perhaps hesitate for a minute, dissatisfied by the sentence, the willed pathos. But what can be done? Shrug, and let the words stand.

Then, further, there's the problem of fame, and how to handle its trophies. The spokesman becoming a celebrity among celebrities need not forsake his cause, isn't obliged to care less than before about his people. But his life circumstances must change. Earlier on, the round of his days could be simply described; no clutter of details associated with conventional success and achievement undercut his protest at the denials of American life. Now, however, he is everywhere undercut. In *No Name in the Street* James Baldwin visits Watts and works in schools—and returns in the afternoon to the Beverly Hills, and condescends to the hotel's ambience in passing (". . . as hotels go, the Beverly Hills is more congenial than most. . . ."). In the Seventies this writer's first-name world embraces not just "Huey" and "Angela" but "Eartha," "Gadge," "Marlon," dozens of the beautiful; his own retinue includes chauffeur and bodyguard; his domiciles multiply; and when, at the close of his book, he dates the work and places its composition, hints of splendor rise from the words: "New York, San Francicso, Hollywood, London, Istanbul, St. Paul de Vence, 1967–1971."

Finally, the spokesman has competition. Is it not tasteless to contend that men compete for recognition as champion voice of agony? Tasteless, yet true. Fame and power are at stake here as elsewhere, and while the writer is concerned not to exalt himself above his cause, he is scarcely an innocent; he feels the others crowding him, bidding for a share of influence. And distraction mounts. Not every commentary on the meaning of the black experience in the Sixties, or earlier, intrudes on the turf marked out by *The Fire Next Time.* Julius Lester's tale of the times, *Search for a New Land,* is more journalistic than apocalyptic; James Foreman's *The Making of Black Revolutionaries* traces intricacies of political infighting among civil-rights groups in a manner that inhibits emotional involvement; and if Harold Cruse's *Crisis of the Negro Intellectual* ranks as a committed work, its tone is historical and scholarly almost to the end, and the personal voice is cool.

But angrier books abound. There's ferocity in Ameer Baraka, and Eldridge Cleaver has gone so far as to attack the author of *Nobody Knows My Name* and to argue straight out, in *Soul on Ice* (1967), that Baldwin's "name" is inflated and his message muddled: "There is in James Baldwin's work the most grueling, total hatred of the blacks, particularly of himself, and the most shameful, fanatical, fawning, sycophantic love of the whites that one can find in the writings of any black American writer of note in our time. This is an appalling contradiction, and the implications of it are vast."

In a word, there's a price for everything, spokesmanship included. The pressures are serious, they build up quickly—and their effect is evident in the work at hand. *No Name in the Street,* a reconstruction of James Baldwin's activities and states of mind during the Sixties (there are glances further backward, and the book ends with President Nixon congratulating Governor Rockefeller on his handling of the Attica uprising), is less powerful, rhetorically, than *The Fire Next Time,* and, although self-referential, contains nothing to match the family remembrances in *Notes of a Native Son.* The writer is restless, rushes himself, seems bored with the drill of conventional dramatization. Much space is given, in the latter portion of the book, to his efforts on behalf of his former bodyguard, Tony Maynard by name, imprisoned on a murder charge; the pages lose force because Maynard, underdone as a character, lays no claim on the audience as a distinct human creature. Much space is also assigned to a projected movie of *The Autobiography of Malcolm X;* these pages lose force because the writer fails to take his reader to the center of the crisis of "control" that led to war with the studio and the decision to abandon the screenplay. Students of James Baldwin's novels will find in the present work a number of images and episodes with interesting bearings on *Go Tell It on the Mountain, Another Country,* even *Giovanni's Room.* But the book as a whole resembles a collection of fragments—snapshots of friends, new snippets about the Harlem boyhood and the down-and-out-in-Paris years, glimpses of the writer on magazine assignment in the South, reports of encounters with Dr. King, Malcolm, Huey Newton. And the unifying ruminations—discursive and historical remarks on the meaning of black-white relationships, predictions about the course of these relationships in the years ahead—don't invariably avoid repetitiousness.

Yet, despite the book's faults, despite the trials and afflictions of his spokesmanship, this author retains a place in an extremely select group: that composed of the few genuinely indispensable American writers. He owes his rank partly to the qualities of responsiveness that have marked his work from the beginning and that seem unlikely ever to disappear from it. Time and time over in fiction as in reportage, Baldwin tears himself free of his rhetorical fastenings and stands forth on the page utterly absorbed in the reality of the person before him, strung with his nerves, riveted to his feelings, breathing his breath. And such moments turn up still in his writing. Here is Baldwin remembering Birmingham, a talk with Reverend Shuttlesworth, an instant at which the minister considers the issue of safety. It's nighttime, early in the voter-registration drive; ahead lie stepped-up bombings, and murders. The two men have been talking together, in Baldwin's hotel room. During the conversation Shuttlesworth keeps walking back and forth to the window. The writer realizes his guest is checking on his car below, making sure nobody puts a bomb in it. He wants to say this, wants to acknowledge the danger and his own awareness of it—but the minister offers him no opening. At last, as Shuttlesworth is leaving, Baldwin speaks out ("I could not resist. . . . I was worried. . . ."), and he sees the man's face change ("a shade of sorrow crossed his face, deep, impatient, dark"), and at once he lives into the response imaginatively, naming it from within, sensing the "impersonal anguish," showing forth the minister wrestling within himself, confronting fear with the almost-sustaining truth that "the danger in which he stood was as nothing compared with the spiritual horror which drove those who were trying to destroy him."

Precisely the same swiftness of penetration occurs as the writer remembers a classic moment of exclusion. He enters a small-town southern restaurant through the "wrong door":

> "What you want, boy? What you want in here?" And then, a decontaminating gesture, "Right around there, boy. Right around there."
>
> I had no idea what [the waitress] was talking about. I backed out the door.
>
> "Right around there, boy," said a voice behind me.
>
> A white man had appeared out of nowhere, on the sidewalk which had been empty not more than a second before. I stared at him blankly. He watched me steadily, with a kind of suspended menace. . . . He had pointed to a door, and I knew immediately that he was pointing to the colored entrance. And this was a dreadful moment—as brief as lightning, and far more illuminating. I realized that this man thought that he was being kind. . . .

Clearly James Baldwin can still take a feeling from inside: Amidst terror, he registers an exact reading of the combined sense of power and inner, *moral* self-approval in the white who shows him "the right way."

But what matters at least as much as this responsiveness is Baldwin's continuing willingness to accept the obligation imposed on him by his pride—namely, that of specifying the losses to the culture as a whole flowing from its blindness to truths born in and taught by blackness. To say this isn't entirely to discount the chronicle aspect of *No Name in the Street*. The narrative is spotty and discontinuous, but it does provide inklings of what it would be like to possess a coherent (although devastatingly despairing) view of recent times, to be able to see even the most dreadful events as part of a pattern. For some citizens the fates of Dr. King, Malcolm X, and Robert Kennedy can be gathered only under a vague rubric ("violence in America," "shocking," "beyond understanding"). Baldwin's narrative is told from the perspective of someone noting connections, replacing soft illusions of randomness with hard-boned inevitabilities, and often justifying his readings by citing particulars not only of his own feelings but of those of the victims. Everywhere in the book linkages are fixed between events that white memories tend to hold apart—witness these comments on the close of the great Washington Monument petitionary march and its sequel:

> Martin finished with one hand raised: "Free at last, free at last, praise God Almighty, I'm free at last!" That day, for a moment, it almost seemed that we stood on a height, and could see our inheritance; perhaps we could make the kingdom real, perhaps the beloved community would not forever remain that dream one dreamed in agony. The people quietly dispersed at nightfall, as had been agreed. . . . I was in Hollywood when, something like two weeks later, my phone rang, and a nearly hysterical, white, female CORE worker told me that a Sunday school in Birmingham had been bombed, and that four young black girls had been blown into eternity. That was the first answer we received to our petition.

Merely by pointing at "sequels," Baldwin bares the structure of the times as given in the experience of his community, and it is a fearful sight.

And it is, to repeat, the author's resources of pride that figure most strikingly in the acts of revelation. True pride is never less than stunning—which is to say, even if it didn't impose obligations, Baldwin's pride would remain a phenomenon notable in itself. These fierce resistances, iron spurnings of every prepared slot of "inferiority"—it is wrong to view them esthetically and thereby drain them of psychological urgency; yet it's hard to gaze on them without remembering Keats's remarks on the "fineness" of a quarrel in the street. The key to excitement in Baldwin's writing is the imminence of contest, the brooding rage to prove self-worth, to duel with the humiliators and cut through to their place of blankness.

And it's his grasp of his comparative worth that demands the duel, forces him into "availability," openness to others; he's driven to perceive inner realities as they exist for persons not himself at least in part because, the system being what it is, others are bound to misassess him, bound to need setting straight. There are no wild moments of release in *No Name in the Street* matching the terrible passage in *Notes of a Native Son* wherein the young Baldwin, told for the thousandth time ". . . don't serve Negroes here," roars up from his chair and hurls a half-full pitcher of water, shattering mirrors behind the bar. The gestures in the name of worth here become gestures of mind, and sometimes take the form of dismissals of traditional culture:

> The South African coal miner, or the African digging for roots in the bush, or the Algerian mason working in Paris, not only have no reason to bow down before Shakespeare, or Descartes, or Westminster Abbey, or the cathedral at Chartres: they have, once these monuments intrude on their attention, no honorable access to them. Their apprehension of this history cannot fail to reveal to them that they have been robbed, maligned, and rejected: to bow down before that history is to accept that history's arrogant and unjust judgment.

The dream of demolishing history is extravagant and in the end self-diminishing; the force of the will, the superb hatred of bowing down nevertheless compels admiration.

But, as just indicated, the prime use of Baldwin's writing is as a guide to fortunes possessed by the dispossessed. Other writers—Frantz Fanon, Albert Memmi, Paolo Freire—hint at the size of the holdings, open up awareness of the way in which a thousand assumptions would be transformed if standard middle-class reality had to negotiate its acceptance with things as they truly are. And these writers exceed James Baldwin in restraint; Baldwin's proud-hearted love of his people often sends him close to euphoric boosting:

> . . . the doctrine of white supremacy, which still controls most white people, is itself a stupendous delusion: but to be born black is an immediate, a mortal challenge. People who cling to their delusions find it difficult, if not impossible, to learn anything worth learning: a people under the necessity of creating themselves must examine everything, and soak up learning the way the roots of a tree soak up water.

But when he lays out his case experientially, it has uncommon authority. "I have been to Watts to give high-school lectures," he writes, and

> these despised, maligned, and menaced children have an alertness, an eagerness, and a depth which I certainly did not find in—or failed to elicit from—students at many splendid universities. The future leaders of this country (in principle, anyway) do not impress me as being the intellectual equals of the most despised among us. I am not being vindictive when I say that, nor am I being sentimental or chauvinistic; and indeed the reason that this would be so is a very simple one. It is only very lately that white students, in the main, have had any reason to question the structure into which they were born; it is the very lateness of the hour, and their bewildered resentment—their sense of having been betrayed—which is responsible for their romantic excesses; and a young, white revolutionary remains, in general, far more romantic than a black one. For it is a very different matter, and results in a very different intelligence, to grow up under the necessity of questioning everything—everything, from the question of one's identity to the literal, brutal question of how to save one's life in order to begin to live it. White children . . . whether they are rich or poor, grow up with a grasp of reality so feeble that they can very accurately be described as deluded—about themselves and the world they live in. . . .

The writer means to create an image of his people that will not only recover their dignity, that will not only spell out what they have to teach, but that will sting all sane folk to jealousy. It is, many will say, adopting postures of regret and pity, a typical "spokesman's project"—and doubtless there's justice in the observation. But the lesson Baldwin teaches in this flawed, bitter, continuously instructive book—you make your way to actualities only by waking to the arbitrariness of things—goes out a few miles beyond "race issues." And those among us who can't or won't master the lesson, or who, having mastered it, carp instead of clap at the pugnacity behind it, had best save the pity for themselves.

Chronology of Important Dates

1924   Born in Harlem Hospital, New York City, August 2, the son
        of Emma Berdis Jones.

1927   Emma Berdis Jones marries David Baldwin.

1935   Graduates from Public School 24 in Harlem.

1937–38 Edits and contributes to school magazine, *The Douglass Pilot.*

1938   Graduates from Frederick Douglass Junior High School (JHS
        139) in Harlem.
        Undergoes religious experience at Mount Calvary of the Pen-
        tecostal Faith Church.

1938–41 Preaches at the Fireside Pentecostal Assembly.

1938–42 Attends De Witt Clinton High School in the Bronx, graduating
        January 29, 1942.

1940–41 Edits and contributes to *The Magpie,* school magazine at De
        Witt Clinton.

1942   Begins first draft of *Go Tell It on the Mountain.*

1942–43 Works in New Jersey and encounters overt white racism.

1943   David Baldwin dies, July 29.

1943–48 Lives and works in Greenwich Village.

1944–45 Meets Richard Wright, who secures for him a Eugene F. Sax-
        ton Memorial Trust Award.

1947   Begins publishing reviews in *The Nation* and *The New
        Leader.*

1948   Rosenwald Fellowship.
        Sails for Europe on a one-way ticket, November 11.

1948–57 Lives in Paris, Switzerland, and the south of France.

1949–50	Meets Lucien Happersberger.
1953	*Go Tell It on the Mountain.*
1954	Guggenheim Fellowship.
1955	*Notes of a Native Son.*
1956	*The Amen Corner* opens at Howard University, with the author attending. Receives a grant from the National Institute of Arts and Letters and a fellowship from *Partisan Review*. *Giovanni's Room.*
1957	Returns in July to the United States to live. Visits the South for the first time in the fall.
1958–59	Works with Elia Kazan at the Actors Studio.
1959	Ford Foundation Grant-in-Aid.
1961	*Nobody Knows My Name.* Drama critic for *The Urbanite*.
1962	*Another Country.*
1963	*The Fire Next Time.* Lectures widely on civil rights. Meets with Attorney General Robert F. Kennedy, May 24. Participates in March on Washington, August 28.
1964	*Blues for Mister Charlie* opens at the ANTA Theatre on Broadway, April 23. *Nothing Personal* (with Richard Avedon).
1965	*Going to Meet the Man.*
1965–67	Lives in Europe and Turkey.
1968	*Tell Me How Long the Train's Been Gone.*
1971	*A Rap on Race* (with Margaret Mead).
1972	*No Name in the Street.*
1973	*One Day, When I was Lost.* *A Dialogue* (with Nikki Giovanni).

Notes on the Editor and Contributors

KENETH KINNAMON, Professor of English at the University of Illinois at Urbana-Champaign, is the author of *The Emergence of Richard Wright: A Study in Literature and Society*. With Richard K. Barksdale he coedited *Black Writers of America: A Comprehensive Anthology*.

CHARLOTTE ALEXANDER has taught at Brooklyn College, New York University, and the City College of the City University of New York.

ROBERT A. BONE of Teachers College, Columbia University, is the author of *The Negro Novel in America*.

ELDRIDGE CLEAVER, writer and revolutionary, is now living in exile. His *Soul on Ice* is a classic of Afro-American literature.

BENJAMIN DEMOTT, the well-known novelist, literary critic, and social observer, teaches at Amherst College and contributes widely to periodicals. His most recent books are *Supergrow* and *Surviving the 70's*.

F. W. DUPEE taught for many years at Columbia University. Among his books are *Henry James* and *"The King of the Cats,"* a collection of literary essays.

MICHEL FABRE of the Sorbonne is the leading French authority on Afro-American culture. Among his books are *Les Noirs américaines, Esclaves et planteurs,* and a definitive biography of Richard Wright recently translated into English.

CALVIN C. HERNTON of the Department of Afro-American Studies at Oberlin College is a sociologist, critic, and poet who has written *Sex and Racism in America, White Papers for White Americans,* and *The Coming of Chronos to the House of Nightsong*.

IRVING HOWE, distinguished critic of literature, politics, and society, teaches at Hunter College and edits *Dissent*. Among his many books are standard studies of Sherwood Anderson, William Faulkner, and Thomas Hardy. Some of his essays have been collected in *Politics and the Novel, A World More Attractive, Steady Work, Decline of the New,* and *The Critical Point*.

165

LANGSTON HUGHES is known best as a major poet and humorist, but in his long and prolific career he also wrote fiction, drama, autobiography, history, and essays, as well as compiling basic anthologies of black poetry and folklore. From the early days of the Harlem Renaissance until his death in 1967, he was at the center of Afro-American literary life.

GEORGE E. KENT is Professor of English at the University of Chicago. *Blackness and the Adventure of Western Culture* includes many of his important essays on black writers. Presently he is at work on a study of William Faulkner.

CHARLES NEWMAN writes fiction (*New Axis* and *The Promisekeeper*), teaches at Northwestern University, and edits *Triquarterly*.

JOHN M. REILLY has written on Baldwin, Wright, Chesnutt, Toomer, and Dos Passos for various journals and has edited *Twentieth Century Interpretations of Invisible Man*. He is Associate Professor of English at the State University of New York at Albany.

SHERLEY ANNE WILLIAMS is a member of the Department of Ethnic Studies at Fresno State College. *Give Birth to Brightness: A Thematic Study in Neo-Black Literature* is her first book.

Selected Bibliography

Breit, Harvey. "James Baldwin and Two Footnotes." In *The Creative Present: Notes on Contemporary American Fiction,* edited by Nona Balakian and Charles Simmons. Garden City, N.Y.: Doubleday, 1963. Pp. 5–24.

Charney, Maurice, "James Baldwin's Quarrel with Richard Wright." *American Quarterly,* 15 (1963), 63–75.

Collier, Eugenia W. "The Phrase Unbearably Repeated." *Phylon,* 25 (1964), 288–96.

————. "Thematic Patterns in Baldwin's Essays." *Black World,* June, 1972, pp. 28–34.

Cox, C. B.; and Jones, A. R. "After the Tranquillized Fifties: Notes on Sylvia Plath and James Baldwin." *The Critical Quarterly,* 6 (1964), 107–22.

Dickstein, Morris. "The Black Aesthetic in White America." *Partisan Review,* 38 (1971), 376–95.

Eckman, Fern Marja. *The Furious Passage of James Baldwin.* New York: M. Evans, 1966.

Finn, James. "The Identity of James Baldwin." *The Commonweal,* October 26, 1962, pp. 113–16.

Foster, David E. " 'Cause my house fell down': The Theme of the Fall in Baldwin's Novels." *Critique,* 13, no. 2 (1971), 50–62.

Gayle, Addison, Jr. "A Defense of James Baldwin." *CLA Journal,* 10 (1967), 201–8.

————. "The Dialectic of 'The Fire Next Time.' " *Negro History Bulletin,* 30 (April, 1967), 15–16.

Gross, Barry. "The 'Uninhabitable Darkness' of Baldwin's *Another Country*: Image and Theme." *Negro American Literature Forum,* 6 (1972), 113–21.

Gross, Theodore L. *The Heroic Ideal in American Literature.* New York: The Free Press, 1971. Pp. 166–79.

Hagopian, John V. "James Baldwin: The Black and the Red-White-and-Blue." *CLA Journal*, 7 (1963), 133–40.

Harper, Howard M., Jr. *Desperate Faith: A Study of Bellow, Salinger, Mailer, Baldwin, and Updike.* Chapel Hill: University of North Carolina Press, 1967. Pp. 137–61.

Howe, Irving. "Black Boys and Native Sons." *Dissent*, 10 (1963), 353–68.

Jacobson, Dan. "James Baldwin as Spokesman." *Commentary*, 32 (1961), 497–502.

Lash, John S. "Baldwin Beside Himself: A Study in Modern Phallicism." *CLA Journal*, 8 (1964), 132–40.

Leaks, Sylvester. "James Baldwin—I Know His Name." *Freedomways*, 3 (1963), 102–5.

Lee, Brian. "James Baldwin: Caliban to Prospero." In *The Black American Writer*, edited by C. W. E. Bigsby. Deland, Fla.: Everett/Edwards, 1969. Vol. 1, pp. 169–79.

Levin, David. "Baldwin's Autobiographical Essays: The Problem of Negro Identity." *The Massachusetts Review*, 5 (1964), 239–47.

Macebuh, Stanley. *James Baldwin: A Critical Study.* New York: The Third Press, 1973.

MacInnes, Colin. "Dark Angel: The Writings of James Baldwin." *Encounter*, August, 1963, pp. 22–33.

Marcus, Steven. "The American Negro in Search of Identity." *Commentary*, 16 (1953), 456–63.

Margolies, Edward. *Native Sons: A Critical Study of Twentieth-Century Negro American Authors.* Philadelphia: J. B. Lippincott Company, 1968. Pp. 102–26.

Mayfield, Julian. "And Then Came Baldwin." *Freedomways*, 3 (1963), 143–55.

Meserve, Walter. "James Baldwin's 'Agony Way.'" In *The Black American Writer*, edited by C. W. E. Bigsby. Deland, Fla.: Everett/Edwards, 1969. Vol. 2, pp. 171–86.

Moore, John Rees. "An Embarrassment of Riches: Baldwin's *Going to Meet the Man.*" *The Hollins Critic*, 2 (December, 1965), 1–12.

Neal, Lawrence P. "The Black Writers' Role: James Baldwin." *Liberator*, April, 1966, pp. 10–11, 18.

Noble, David W. *The Eternal Adam and the New World Garden: The Central Myth in the American Novel Since 1830.* New York: George Braziller, 1968. Pp. 209–17.

O'Brien, Conor Cruise. "White Gods and Black Americans." *New Statesman*, May 1, 1964, pp. 681–82.

Roth, Philip. "Channel X: Two Plays on the Race Conflict." *The New York Review of Books,* May 28, 1964, pp. 10–13.

Sayre, Robert F. "James Baldwin's Other Country." In *Contemporary American Novelists,* edited by Harry T. Moore. Carbondale: Southern Illinois University Press, 1964. Pp. 158–69.

Scott, Nathan A., Jr. "Judgment Marked by a Cellar: The American Negro Writer and the Dialectic of Despair." *The Denver Quarterly,* 2 (Summer, 1967), 5–35.

Simmons, Harvey G. "James Baldwin and the Negro Conundrum." *The Antioch Review,* 23 (1963), 250–55.

Spender, Stephen. "James Baldwin: Voice of a Revolution." *Partisan Review,* 30 (1963), 256–60.

Standley, Fred L. "*Another Country,* Another Time." *Studies in the Novel,* 4 (1972), 504–12.

———. "James Baldwin: The Artist as Incorrigible Disturber of the Peace." *Southern Humanities Review,* 4 (1970), 18–30.

———. "James Baldwin: The Crucial Situation." *The South Atlantic Quarterly,* 65 (1966), 371–81.

Thelwell, Mike. "*Another Country:* Baldwin's New York Novel." In *The Black American Writer,* edited by C. W. E. Bigsby. Deland, Fla.: Everett/Edwards, 1969. Vol. 1, pp. 181–98.

Wills, Garry. "What Color Is God?" *National Review,* 14 (1963), 408–14, 416–17.

TWENTIETH CENTURY VIEWS

American Authors

TWENTIETH CENTURY VIEWS

British Authors

(continued on next page)

(*continued from previous page*)

TWENTIETH CENTURY VIEWS

European Authors